BUTTERFLY
Gardening

BUTTERFLY
Gardening

Creating A
Butterfly
Haven in
Your Garden

Thomas C. Emmel, Ph. D.

FRIEDMAN/FAIRFAX
PUBLISHERS

A FRIEDMAN/FAIRFAX BOOK

Library of Congress Cataloging-in-Publication Data

Emmel, Thomas C.
      Butterfly gardening : creating a butterfly haven in your garden / Thomas C. Emmel.
                  p.   cm.
      Includes bibliographical references and index.
      ISBN 1-56799-525-X
      1. Butterfly gardening—North America. 2. Butterflies—North America—Identification.I. Title.
      QL544.6.E47 1997
      635.9'67—dc21   96—40512

Editor: Celeste Sollod
Book Designed by: ico-nol-o-gy graphics Pamela E. Mitchell
Art Director: Jeff Batzli
Photography Editor: Kathryn Culley
Production Manager: Camille Lee

Color separations by Ocean Graphic International Company Ltd.
Printed in Singapore by KHL Printing Co Pte Ltd.

1 3 5 7 9 10 8 6 4 2

For bulk purchases and special sales, please contact:
Friedman/Fairfax Publishers
Attention: Sales Department
15 West 26th Street
New York, New York 10010
212/685-6610   FAX 212/685-1307

Visit our website:
http://www.metrobooks.com

DEDICATION

This book is dedicated to three outstanding pioneers in butterfly gardening, who together have done more than any others in the world to directly influence hundreds of thousands of people a year to consider butterfly gardening as an avocation or even a vocation. Mr. Ronald Boender, founder and director of Butterfly World in Coconut Creek, Florida, has not only brought the joys of butterflies and their fascinating lives home to millions of visitors but has also developed weekly seminar programs of instruction at Butterfly World, television programs on butterfly gardening, and most recently, his nationwide campaign to Bring Back the Butterflies, which includes lists of appropriate nectar sources and caterpillar food plants for species in each region of the United States. Mr. Clive P. Farrell, co-partner with Ron Boender in founding Butterfly World and developer of butterfly exhibits and farms throughout the United Kingdom, has likewise introduced millions of Europeans to the joys of butterflies and gardening especially for them. Along with Ron Boender, he has encouraged butterfly farmers to raise butterflies in many parts of the world. Finally, Mrs. Deen Day Smith of Georgia played the instrumental role in founding the Day Butterfly Center at Callaway Gardens, Georgia, where more than 600,000 visitors a year can see the fascination of living butterflies and learn gardening techniques to attract them. Working with the Garden Clubs of America, she has spread the message of butterfly gardening not only throughout Georgia but across America. To all three of these individuals, whose efforts have been unstinting and vastly influential in promoting butterfly gardening, this book is dedicated.

ACKNOWLEDGMENTS

I wish to thank Sharyn Rosart, Editorial Director of Michael Friedman Publishing Group, Inc., for her inspiration and careful, nurturing development of this project. Ronald and Grace Boender of Butterfly World in Florida have been the chief inspiration for my involvement in butterfly gardening; of course, their influence is being felt throughout North America and indeed the rest of the world as they carry their message of "bringing back the butterflies" to a great many people and every continent through their example, media dissemination, and direct help for butterfly farmers. Countless other lepidopterists have contributed to the material in this book in ways too numerous to list here, but sincere thanks go to all. Christine and Peter Eliazar criticized the manuscript and offered helpful suggestions. Christine Eliazar prepared the manuscript in her usual outstanding manner.

CONTENTS

CHAPTER ONE

A Short History of Butterfly Gardening

utterfly gardening in North America is a relatively recent phenomenon. Although butterflies live almost everywhere and there are some 765 species flying north of Mexico throughout the United States and Canada, it wasn't until the late 1980s that an explosion of interest in planting gardens specifically to attract butterflies began. Now, hundreds of thousands of people a year are discovering the pleasures and fascination of butterfly gardening. This book is designed to help you, too, discover how to attract the maximum number of species and individual butterflies to your garden. It doesn't matter if you are a beginning gardener or a highly advanced one; *Butterfly Gardening* will provide you with

Blackfoot Daisy (*Melampodium leucanthum*), a low-mounded perennial covered with white daisy-like flowers, grows well in full sun. Here it is planted in front of *Pennisetum seta*.

everything you need to develop a truly beautiful, even spectacular, showplace for you, your family, and your friends to enjoy for many years (to say nothing of the butterflies' enjoyment!).

To a certain degree, butterfly gardening has probably been around for at least a century. English butterfly books are replete with advice on planting caterpillar food plants and leaving some parts of English estates wild to attract butterflies. L. Hugh Freeman, a British butterfly enthusiast, developed the first major butterfly farm in England early in the twentieth century and sold eggs and butterflies at other stages of their life cycles to enthusiasts throughout Europe. Having published several books and many articles on his discoveries in butterfly gardening, Freeman was asked to plant a butterfly garden at the estate of Sir Winston Churchill, Prime Minister of England, where the leader could retreat for a few hours from the nonstop cares of guiding the country through the perilous times of World War II. In the late 1970s, Clive P. Farrell began developing a series of butterfly exhibit houses and farms where people can see living butterflies by the thousands, even in the middle of the coldest winter months.

Inspired by these English examples, butterfly farming and gardening was brought to America in the early 1980s. Ronald Boender, a recently retired businessman, founded MetaScience, Inc., in Ft. Lauderdale, Florida, to breed butterflies on a large scale and supply them to colleges, universities, and researchers working with Lepidoptera, the order of insects encompassing moths and butterflies. Starting in his screened pool enclosure and spreading to specially designed enclosures, Boender soon had a vision of a great butterfly garden complex, complete with enclosures where free-flying butterflies could be observed close at hand by visitors. In May 1988, Butterfly World, a three-acre complex devoted to raising and displaying living butterflies and some of their more spectacular moth relatives, opened to the public at Coconut Creek, just north of Ft. Lauderdale in southern Florida. Four months later, in September 1988, the Day Butterfly Center opened at Callaway Gardens in Georgia, the product of another inspired individual, Deen Day Smith, whose enthusiasm for butterflies led her to found this center for the enjoyment of the general public. Mrs. Smith's extensive involvement in the Garden Clubs of America has spread the message of butterfly gardening throughout hundreds of chapters of this outstanding organization and to their membership nationwide.

From the initial enthusiasm generated across North America by the first butterfly houses has come the development of dozens of additional butterfly displays at major public zoos, museums, open-air animal exhibits, public gardens, and private gardens. A major new society of amateur enthusiasts for study of living Lepidoptera, especially in gardens and nature, The North American Butterfly Association, was founded by Jeffrey A. Glassberg, a well-known molecular geneticist and businessman. In just four years, NABA has passed a membership of two thousand people. Its bimonthly journal contains many color-illustrated articles pertaining to butterfly gardening and preserving natural habitats for butterflies.

The wave of enthusiasm for butterfly gardening now sweeping the country has resulted in the media paying much attention to butterflies. From a multitude of stories on endangered species, such as the Schaus Swallowtail in south Florida and the Florida Keys, to butterflies being threatened

Echinacea **composites mixed with grasses will bring a variety of butterflies to the garden.**

Mustards in the genus *Brassica* will attract Orange tips, Marbles, and Whites to your garden.

Porcupine grass (*Miscanthus sinensis*) from China is effectively used here at the Longwood Gardens in Kennett Square, Pennsylvania, to provide a dramatic accent in a garden bed.

by a giant reservoir project near the city of Denver, butterflies have played an important role in calling people's attention to the importance of preserving the environment and the balance of nature. Each fall, thousands of classrooms across the country order Monarch butterfly larvae or Painted Lady caterpillars to watch the endlessly fascinating saga of metamorphosis take place before their eyes. Thousands of amateurs and professionals have joined together to band Monarch butterflies each fall to contribute toward learning more about these butterflies' incredible migration habits. Butterfly aficionados also work to preserve the Monarchs' overwintering sites in California and central Mexico.

New local societies form monthly across the United States and Canada for butterfly enthusiasts to join and share their experiences with Lepidoptera. All this newfound enthusiasm for butterflying and butterfly gardening is similar to how birding and the study of North American birds became popular in the 1930s due to the first field guides by Roger Tory Peterson and the knowledge that birding could be enjoyed by anyone with binoculars. Today, butterflying can be enjoyed by anyone with binoculars, especially those who wish to plant butterfly gardens and bring some of these fascinating creatures to their home environments every day.

Butterfly Gardening is planned to help you organize your garden design and develop a butterfly garden appropriate to your home area and your local environment. You will also be able to learn how to identify the butterflies that come to your garden and watch them with greater understanding, from the tips, techniques, and equipment that are described in the following chapters.

Masses of composites of several species—including Korean hybrid chrysanthemums, Dendranthema × zawadskii (D. × grandiflorum), Ageratum, and grasses—are shown at the New York Botanical Garden in the Bronx, New York. Butterflies respond to such masses much more effectively than to isolated plants.

CHAPTER TWO

Planning Your Butterfly Garden

Planning a butterfly garden is one of the most enjoyable and least expensive leisure-time activities you can undertake. You have the opportunity to start something new in your existing yard or garden—with a fresh variety of plants, a fresh design, and fresh goals and boundless enjoyment ahead of you. The results you will achieve are really limited only by the amount of space and time you can devote to this project, for you can readily propagate many of the desired plants from just a few "starter" plants to achieve the desired results.

Your garden can be as simple or as elaborate as you want, designed for just a few species of butterflies that particularly

A Dainty Yellow visits a Blanketflower bloom (*Gaillardia*). This plant puts out brightly colored orange and red flowers all summer.

interest you or for the widest variety possible. You can provide your butterflies solely with nectar sources, and see immediate results by attracting them in just a few minutes for temporary visits. Or even better, you can add larval host plants for the caterpillars, plants which will bring male and female butterflies to breed in your garden, to court in elaborate dancing flight and mating displays, followed by egg-laying and the rich unfolding of the butterfly's life history before your eyes. You can even provide water in the form of streams, ponds, and waterfalls, with special watering "beaches" of moist sand for Swallowtails and Sulphurs to drink from. If you get particularly ambitious (or have the right terrain in your backyard), you can have

a rocky crag, with trees of various kinds attracting special species with extraordinarily interesting behavioral repertoires that will provide endless hours of fascination for you in your garden.

HOW AND WHAT TO PLANT

When most gardening lepidopterists first think of the words "butterfly garden," they think of nectar sources—plants that have a rich array of colorful blooms and abundant nectar in deep-throated flowers, which provide attractive sipping pleasure for adult butterflies. But these nectar sources are not the only needs for a butterfly garden. We also want to consider the placement of larval host plants so that the butterflies can reproduce in

our gardens and have their eggs, caterpillars, and pupae go through their whole life cycle there. We want to allow many species to develop into permanent residents of our butterfly garden. So let's consider each of these types of plants in turn.

Nectar Sources

Nectar sources are the colorful, showy-flowered plants that provide a sweet-scented nectar that contains the right amount of dissolved sugar to attract butterflies over other pollinators, such as bees or hummingbirds. Butterfly-pollinated plants are usually red or other warm colors like orange or yellow, have a sweet odor that attracts these insects to these flowers for a nectar reward, and usually

Red violets (*Viola*) bloom in a Colorado mountain garden at Breckenridge. The violets serve as larval foodplants for Fritillary butterflies of the genus *Speyeria*.

Fruit tree species of the genus *Prunus* (Japanese cherry shown here) serve as caterpillar foodplants for some of our most attractive Swallowtails as well as providing a beautiful display of flowers in the springtime.

possess flowers which are large enough to provide a landing platform for the butterfly to settle on while feeding.

If you are planning to use native plants for attracting butterflies, your best bet is to go out on the trails and byways of your local parks or other wild areas and see what the butterflies themselves are choosing in your area. Do they like milkweeds? Are they coming to flowering wild rhododendrons? Or are they flying to wild daisies or other composites, mints, or thistles? By noting which plants the widest variety of species are visiting, you can return to those plants later in the season when they have gone to seed, and harvest some of the seeds for your garden. It is usually prohibited to dig up wildflower plants and transplant them to your garden: Be sure to check local and state laws regulating wildflower collection, even of seed. Native plants usually wilt if they are dug out of their

native habitat, and rarely recover into vigorous growth if moved in such a fashion. Alternatively, you can go to a nursery in your area that specializes in offering native plants already potted and growing, and save a lot of work and time by getting healthy, already-started plants to put out in your garden.

If you live in the middle of a large city or there are other reasons that native plants are unavailable, then the larger nurseries in your area should have a section of nursery-grown butterfly gardening plants, or be willing to order some for you. Most retail nurseries and garden centers are anxious to supply the plants that their clients want, and if you and your friends take up butterfly gardening, the local nurserymen will certainly respond to the demand in short order if they have no appropriate plants in stock.

What kinds of standard nectar-source plants are available commercially? In virtually

all sections of the country, you can obtain lantana plants with variously colored flowers, and these are excellent nectar sources. Pick the low-growing shrub varieties with light-colored flowers, if possible; tan- and orange-flowered lantana plants will attract the maximum diversity of butterflies, although purple-flowered lantana is good for Skippers and certain other species. Lantana will bloom most of the year and is a perennial in the warm parts of the United States.

Most nurseries in the southern half of the country will also sell pentas starting in late spring. Pentas are perennial plants that come in a variety of flower colors. The red-flowered forms and white-flowered varieties are the most attractive to butterflies, but any color (pink, purple, etc.) will do the job. Pentas are wonderful perennials that can be planted as annuals (to be replaced each year) in northern climes, and they will attract but-

TABLE ONE

NECTAR SOURCES FOR AMERICAN AND CANADIAN BUTTERFLIES

AGERATUM
(Ageratum houstonianum)
Cabbage White, Checkered White, Blues, Hairstreaks, Skippers

ALFALFA *(Medicago sativa)*
Orange Sulphur, Eastern Black Swallowtail, Checkered White

ASTER *(Aster species)*
Western Tiger Swallowtail, Checkered White, Orange Sulphur, Common Sulphur, Checkerspots, Crescentspots, Question Mark, Painted Lady, American Painted Lady, Red Admiral, Buckeye, Blues, Hairstreaks, Fiery Skipper, Checkered Skipper, other Skipper species

BEGGAR-TICKS *(Bidens alba and other species)*
Cloudless Giant Sulphur, Barred Sulphur, Sleepy Orange, Monarch, Queens, Gulf Fritillary, Zebra Heliconian, Julia, Buckeye, Red Admiral, Painted Lady, Hairstreaks such as Sweadner's Hairstreak and Olive Hairstreak, Blues, Long-Tailed Skippers, Fiery Skipper, and other Skipper species

BUTTERFLY BUSH
(Buddleia davidii and related species)
Anise Swallowtail, Western Tiger Swallowtail, Pale Swallowtail, Eastern Tiger Swallowtail, Danaus Swallowtail, Pipevine Swallowtail, Giant Swallowtail, Spicebush Swallowtail, Palamedes Swallowtail, Monarch, Queens, Viceroy, Red-Spotted Purple, Comma, Question Mark, Painted Lady, American Painted Lady, many Hairstreaks, many Skippers, Cloudless Giant Sulphur

BUTTERFLY WEED *(Asclepias tuberosa)*
Eastern Tiger Swallowtail, Western Tiger Swallowtail, Giant Swallowtail, Spicebush Swallowtail, Palamedes Swallowtail, Pipevine Swallowtail, Cabbage White, Checkered White, Orange Sulphur, Common Sulphur, Monarch, Queens, Viceroy, Question Mark, Painted Lady, American Painted Lady, Red Admiral, Great Purple Hairstreak, Gray Hairstreak and other Hairstreaks, Spring Azure and other Blues, Fiery Skipper and other Skippers

BUTTONBUSH
(Cephalanthus species)
Eastern Tiger Swallowtail, Monarch, Painted Lady, American Painted Lady

CALIFORNIA WILD LILAC
(Ceanothus species)
Pale Swallowtail, Western Tiger Swallowtail

DAISY
(Chrysanthemum species)
Fiery Skipper, Long-Tailed Skipper

DANDELION
(Taraxacum officinale)
Cabbage White, Common Sulphur, Comma, Fiery Skipper

DOGBANE
(Apocynum species)
A great variety of Hairstreaks, Blues such as Spring Azure, Swallowtails, Whites, Sulphurs, Buckeye, American Painted Lady, Skippers

FLEABANE *(Aster species)*
Checkerspots, Crescentspots, Whites, Orangetips, Ringlets, Skippers

GOLDENROD
(Solidago species)
Orange Sulphur, Common Sulphur, Checkerspots, Fritillaries, American Painted Lady, Hairstreaks, Blues, Monarch

HELIOTROPE
(Heliotropium arborescens)
Blues, Skippers, Hairstreaks

IRONWEED
(Vernonia species)
Eastern Tiger Swallowtail, Spicebush Swallowtail, Monarch, Great Spangled Fritillary and other Fritillaries, Fiery Skipper and other Skippers

KNAPWEED
(Centaurea species)
Common Sulphur, Painted Lady, American Painted Lady, Fiery Skipper and other Skippers

LANTANA
(Lantana camara and related species)
A wide variety of Swallowtails, Sulphurs, Whites, Nymphalids such as the Gulf Fritillary, Fiery Skipper and other Skippers

LILAC
(Syringa species and hybrids)
Eastern Tiger Swallowtail, Spring Azure

LOCOWEED
(Oxytropis species)
Blues, Sulphurs

LUPINE *(Lupinus species)*
Blues, Gray Hairstreak

MALLOWS *(Malva species)*
Monarch, Red Admiral, Painted Lady, American Painted Lady, Western Pygmy Blue and other Blues, Skippers such as the Checkered Skippers

MILKWEED
(Asclepias species, especially orange-flowered subspecies*)* Eastern Tiger Swallowtail, Western Tiger Swallowtail, Giant Swallowtail, Spicebush Swallowtail, Palamedes Swallowtail, Pipevine Swallowtail, Cabbage White, Checkered White, Orange Sulphur, Common Sulphur, Monarch, Queens, Viceroy, Question Mark, Painted Lady, American Painted Lady, Red Admiral, Great Purple Hairstreak, Gray Hairstreak and other Hairstreaks, Spring Azure and other Blues, Fiery Skipper and other Skippers

MINT *(Mentha* species*)* Anise Swallowtail, Baird's Swallowtail, Western Tiger Swallowtail, Cabbage White, Checkered White, Monarch, Red Admiral, Painted Lady, American Painted Lady, Gray Hairstreak

MOUNTAIN MINT *(Monardella odoratissima)* Fritillaries, Checkerspots

PEARLY EVERLASTING *(Anaphalis margaritacea)* Painted Lady, American Painted Lady

PRIVET *(Ligustrum* species*)* American Painted Lady, Gray Hairstreak, Spring Azure Blue, Silver-Spotted Skipper

PURPLE CONEFLOWER *(Echinacea* species*)* Great Spangled Fritillary and other Fritillaries, Painted Lady, American Painted Lady, Red Admiral, Gray Hairstreak and other Hairstreaks

QUEEN ANNE'S LACE *(Daucus carota* var. *carota)* Eastern Black Swallowtail, Diana Fritillary, Bog Fritillary, Gray Hairstreak and other Hairstreaks, Crescentspots, Checkerspots

RED CLOVER *(Trifolium pratense)* Checkered White, Cabbage White, Red Admiral, Painted Lady, American Painted Lady, Great Spangled Fritillary and other Fritillaries, Acmon Blue and other Blues, Silver-Spotted Skipper, Checkered Skippers, Fiery Skipper

RUDBECKIA *(Rudbeckia* species, especially Black-Eyed Susan *(Rudbeckia hirta)* Fritillaries, Checkered White, Dwarf Yellow, Blues, Hairstreaks, Skippers

SEDUM *(Sedum spectabile)* Checkered White, Cabbage White, many Nymphalids, and Skippers

SELF-HEAL *(Prunella* species*)* Cabbage White, American Painted Lady, Silver-Spotted Skipper

SPICEBUSH *(Lindera benzoin)* Spicebush Swallowtail, Pipevine Swallowtail, Eastern Tiger Swallowtail

SWEET PEA *(Lathyrus odoratus)* Gray Hairstreak

THISTLE *(Cirsium* species*)* Western Tiger Swallowtail, Eastern Tiger Swallowtail, Spicebush Swallowtail, Pipevine Swallowtail, Red Admiral, Painted Lady, American Painted Lady, Gulf Fritillary, Zebra Heliconian, Fritillaries, Checkerspots, Crescentspots, Monarch, Sulphurs, Whites, Hairstreaks, many Skipper species

TICKSEED *(Coreopsis grandiflora)* Orange Sulphur, Common Sulphur, Monarch, Buckeye

VERBENA *(Verbena* and related species*)* Skippers, Sulphurs, Great Spangled Fritillary

VETCH *(Vicia* species*)* American Painted Lady, Blues of various species

VIOLET *(Viola* species*)* Spring Azure

WHITE SWEET CLOVER *(Melilotus alba)* Many species of Blues, Sulphurs, Skippers

WINTER CRESS *(Barbarea* species*)* Checkered White, Cabbage White, Falcate Orangetip, Spring Azure Blue, Gray Hairstreak, Silver-Spotted Skipper

WORMWOOD or SAGEBRUSH *(Artemisia* species*)* Eastern Tiger Swallowtail, Monarch, Great Spangled Fritillary

YARROW *(Achillea millefolium)* Checkerspots, Crescentspots, Blues, Whites, Hairstreaks, Skippers

ZINNIA *(Zinnia elegans)* Skippers, many Nymphalids, Swallowtails

Top: *Zinnia elegans* and other zinnias are good nectar sources for a great many butterfly species and bloom throughout the spring and summer months.
Bottom: The bright colors of *Salvia vanhoutii* and a Korean hybrid chrysanthemum (*Dendranthema* × *zawadskii* (*D.* × *grandiflorum*) form an attractive mixture to bring butterflies into the garden.

terflies from midspring to the end of fall as they bloom continuously with abundant flower clusters at the top of each multiple-branched shoot.

Another good group of plants includes all the *Verbena* species. Nurseries in various parts of North America have different species of verbena plants: some tall, some short in height and with prostrate or spreading growth, others medium-size and densely flowered. All will attract many beautiful butterflies throughout their long blooming period each year.

Salvia is a good, attractive flower to have in the garden for ornamental purposes. Plant it in masses and it will bring in great numbers of Sulphurs and Swallowtails, if you pick a red-flowered variety with good nectar (some of the commercial varieties lack significant nectar production, and the butterfly will come to the flower but leave in a second or two after it discovers the lack of nectar!). The purple varieties are attractive to bees but not to many butterflies.

Various mints are also being offered by more and more nurseries now, and these are especially attractive to nymphalid butterflies like Fritillaries, and also Swallowtails and even Hairstreaks. Native mints such as those in the genus *Monardella* (especially the species *M. odoratissima*) are easily grown from seed gathered in the wild and make an attractive addition to your garden.

Impatiens is a worldwide genus of tropical and subtropical plants that is widely available now in North American nurseries. It comes in a wonderful array of flower types and colors, and many hybrid varieties are available. We have found the red and orange strains to be most attractive to butterflies in California and in the southern United States, but you can try masses (groups of ten or more plants) of other colors such as pink and white on your local butterflies.

Porterweed is a tall, pantropical weed that comes in various colors such as deep purple, blue, and even pink. It is very attractive to Skippers and certain other butterflies. Zinnias, natives of Africa, are widely used in cultivation in North America and are an excellent source of nectar for many butterfly species. You can plant these in front of higher growing species of nectar plants and achieve a marvelous array of colors in your butterfly garden. Marigolds make nice border plants at the front of your garden, and will attract numerous Skippers while also providing a repellent barrier to some garden pests which dislike its odor!

Left: Mustards, such as *Brassica juncea*, are host plants for some of the butterflies known as Whites, especially the Cabbage White.
Above: A monarch feeds on *Buddleia davidii* 'Dubonnet'. This hardy perennial shrub is also attractive to a great many other butterflies and can be grown in almost any part of the North America.

Heliotrope (especially genus *Heliotropium*) comes in several species of, normally white, small-flowered plants that are very attractive to most butterflies. The large shrubs in the genus *Buddleia*, also called butterfly bush, are found in U.S. and Canadian nurseries. Several species may be offered; *B. davidii* is particularly good for the butterfly garden. If you get a white-or light blue-colored cultivar, you will be amazed at the number of butterflies that swarm to your buddleia bushes throughout the late summer and fall months. The darker purple-flowered buddleia shrubs are quite attractive to butterflies such as Skippers and Sulphurs, but do not normally bring in as many butterflies as the lighter colored buddleias.

If you go to your local plant nursery on a warm sunny day and just watch the various flowering plants there for a while, you may discover other potentially great species for your garden that your particular nursery has stocked for sale. Note whether the butterflies are visiting these or not, and what species are coming. For example, your nursery may have some *Sedum spectabile*, a stonecrop succulent species with a very attractive broad flower head that pulls in many butterflies. They may have temperate and tropical species of milkweeds, such as *Asclepias curassavica*, available for sale. Any plants like this that are regionally available are worth getting and adding to the diversity in your garden.

Larval Hosts

If you choose to plant only the attractive flowering nectar sources at your home, your butterflies will soon move on to other areas in search of places to lay their eggs, leaving your garden. Also, you won't have the pleasure of increasing the number of butterflies in your area if you provide no food for the developing early stages. Thus, it is wise to plan on devoting at least a section of your garden to larval host plants that the female adults will lay eggs on, and that the developing caterpillars will happily feed on to reach the pupal stage (which will subsequently hatch into adults that call your garden "home"). Male butterflies will come into your garden in search of the females and you may even see them stay around the host plants, waiting for fresh females to emerge from pupae or older females to arrive in search of egg-laying sites. Thus, adding larval host plants to your garden can be your genuinely valuable yearly contribution to bringing back large numbers of butterflies to urban areas of North America.

The best way to decide on host plants for your garden is to read about the species of butterflies you wish to attract and what their larval host plants are (see chapter 6). These potential hosts will differ for each region of the country, depending on what butterfly species are in your area, of course. But there are some groups of plants that are used generally by related butterfly species across the country and you can add these as standard food plants to your garden with a practical guarantee of attracting one or more butterfly species to lay their eggs on your offering.

A Japanese flowering cherry (*Prunus jamasakura*) forms an effective backdrop to the early spring flowers in a butterfly garden.

TABLE TWO

LARVAL HOST PLANTS FOR SOME COMMON AMERICAN AND CANADIAN BUTTERFLIES

ALFALFA *(Medicago sativa)*
Orange Sulphur

APPLE *(Malus species)*
Spring Azure Blue

ASTER *(Aster species)*
Checkerspots

BEANS *(Phaseolus species)*
Gray Hairstreak,
Silver-Spotted Skipper

CABBAGE *(Brassica oleracea var. capitata)*
Cabbage White

CARROT *(Daucus carota)*
Anise Swallowtail, Eastern Black
Swallowtail

CHERRY *(Prunus species)*
Eastern Tiger Swallowtail

CUDWEED
(Gnaphalium species)
American Painted Lady

DOGWOOD
(Cornus species)
Spring Azure Blue

EVERLASTING *(Anaphalis species, Antennaria species)*
American Painted Lady

FALSE FOXGLOVE
(Aureolaria pedicularia)
Buckeye

HOLLYHOCK
(Alcea species)
Painted Lady, Common
Checkered Skipper

INDIAN PAINTBRUSH
(Castilleja species)
Checkerspots (Euphydryas and
Chlosyne species)

IRONWEED
(Vernonia species)
American Painted Lady

KNAPWEED
(Centaurea species)
Painted Lady

LUPINE *(Lupinus species)*
Blues

MALLOW *(Malva species)*
Painted Lady, West Coast Lady,
Gray Hairstreak

MILKWEEDS
(Asclepias species)
Monarch, Queens

MUSTARD
(Brassica species)
Cabbage White, Checkered
White

PARSLEY
(Petroselinum crispum)
Anise Swallowtail, Eastern
Black Swallowtail

PASSIONFLOWER
(Passiflora species)
Gulf Fritillary, Zebra Heliconian,
Julia

PLANTAIN
(Plantago species)
Buckeye, Edith's Checkerspot,
Bay Area Checkerspot

QUEEN ANNE'S LACE
(Daucus carota var. carota)
Eastern Black Swallowtail

STINGING NETTLE
(Urtica dioica)
Milbert's Tortoiseshell,
Red Admiral

SWEET PEA
(Lathyrus odoratus)
Gray Hairstreak

THISTLE *(Cirsium species)*
Painted Lady

VETCH *(Vicia species)*
Common Sulphur, Orange
Sulphur, Gray Hairstreak, Blues

VIOLET *(Viola species)*
Fritillaries, such as Diana and
Great Spangled Fritillaries

WILLOW *(Salix species)*
Western Tiger Swallowtail,
Eastern Tiger Swallowtail,
Viceroy, Red-Spotted Purple

WINTER CRESS
(Barbarea species)
Cabbage White, Checkered
White, Spring Azure Blue

WISTERIA *(Wisteria species)*
Silver-Spotted Skipper

WOOD NETTLE
(Laportea canadensis)
Red Admiral, Comma

**WORMWOOD
OR SAGEBRUSH**
(Artemisia species)
Oregon Swallowtail, Baird's
Swallowtail, Alaskan Machaon
Swallowtail, American
Painted Lady

Thus, for example, try planting willows (*Salix* species), aspens and poplars (*Populus* species), and wild plums and cherries (*Prunus* species) to attract Swallowtails like the Western Tiger Swallowtail, Pale Swallowtail, Lorquin's Admiral, Mourning Cloak, Viceroy, Eastern Tiger Swallowtail, Red-spotted Purple, and those representing other large, colorful, and spectacular species. You can plant fennel, parsley, carrot, or dill to attract the Anise Swallowtail in the western United States and the Black Swallowtail in the eastern United States. If you put out spicebush or sassafras in the southeastern United States, or even the Northeast, you can get the Spicebush Swallowtail in numbers. Try planting some pipevine in central California, Arizona, and across the southern tier of states, and you will soon have

Top: Dill (*Ruta graveolens*) is a member of the Rutaceae family which is chemically very similar to the members of the parsley family (Umbelliferae) and is used as a larval foodplant by the Black Swallowtail and its relatives.
Bottom: Nasturtium (*Tropaeolum majus* 'Tip Top Apricot') is a nice colorful border plant which will attract Cabbage Whites and their relatives and serve as a larval foodplant for them.

Pipevine Swallowtails inhabiting your garden with their brilliant blue-purple-black iridescence. In Florida, you will also have the Polydamus Swallowtail (a yellow-spotted, iridescent greenish-black species) coming to your pipevines.

Then try some weedy plants, such as milkweeds for the Monarch and two Queen species, or wild senna (*Cassia* species) for Cloudless Sulphurs and their many Sulphur relatives. Plant a variety of passionflower vines from California to the Gulf states, and you can expect to get the Gulf Fritillary in abundance in your garden. Further south in Florida, your passionflower vines will also attract the Zebra Heliconian and perhaps even the Julia, a bright orange, fast-flying, long-winged Heliconian butterfly.

If you plant a variety of asters, you may attract the various Crescentspots in the genus *Phyciodes*, such as the Pearl Crescent, or the larger Checkerspots in the genus *Chlosyne*. If you plant a lot of snapdragons and verbena in your garden, virtually anywhere across North America, you will probably attract the Buckeye (*Junonia coenia*). The common Cabbage White butterfly will happily lay eggs on the garden nasturtium, and its larvae will feed on it in a series of new generations throughout the year until the winter frosts. You can also plant yellow mustard (*Brassica* species) to attract the Cabbage White and other whites to take up permanent residence in your garden.

If you plant a variety of violet species, you may attract a local Fritillary species in the genus *Speyeria*, such as the Great Spangled Fritillary, to lay its eggs and start a colony in your backyard. If in your lawn or around your border you plant lippia, you may attract the Phaon Crescentspot to feed on it. Plant a variety of grasses and allow

Wheatgrass mixed with wildflowers in a Tucson garden in the springtime (which blooms again during late summer rains) will attract a surprising variety of butterflies, bees, and other pollinating insects.

Top left: Parsley is very attractive to the Eastern Black Swallowtail (*Papilio polyxenes*) as a larval foodplant and can be planted as a foliage border along the edges of paths in the butterfly garden.

Right: A red passionvine (*Passiflora coccinea*), here growing in the Selby Botanical Gardens at Sarasota, Florida, is an attractive host plant for the Gulf Fritillary, the Zebra Heliconian, and the Julia in the South.

them grow up in clumps and even go to seed, and you will attract grass-feeding Satyrid butterflies and Skippers that have grasses as their larval food plants.

The list of potential food plants is really almost endless, especially if you also want to attract moths (there are more than ten times as many moth species as butterflies!). Just read the gallery of butterflies section, chapter 6, for ideas on other food plants to try in your garden, and look up some of the recommended butterfly identification manuals which are available at your local library to get additional ideas on food plants to establish on your soil.

GENERAL BUTTERFLY GARDEN DESIGN
FOR RECTANGULAR FRONT AND BACK YARDS

1. **Aspens or Birches** (cool areas), **Crape Myrtles** (southern areas)
2. **Liriodendrons** (tulip trees)
3. **Elms**
4. **Willows**
5. **Sassafras**
6. **Rudbeckias**
7. **Buddleias**
8. **Hollyhocks**
9. **Shasta Daisies**
10. **Asters**
11. **Red impatiens**
12. **White impatiens**
13. **Bracken Ferns**
14. **Pink Impatiens**
15. **Plantagos**
16. **Purple or White Thistles**
17. **Red Pentas**
18. **Red, Purple, White, Salvias**
19. **Snapdragons**
20. **Purple verbenas**
21. **Lantanas**
22. **Passionflowers**
23. **Cassias** (yellow flowers)
24. **Milkweeds** (*Asclepias curassavicca* or other species)
25. **Giant Alliums** (onions)
26. **Ageratums** (purple)
27. **Sweet Peas** (on trellis)
28. **Violets** (*Viola* species)

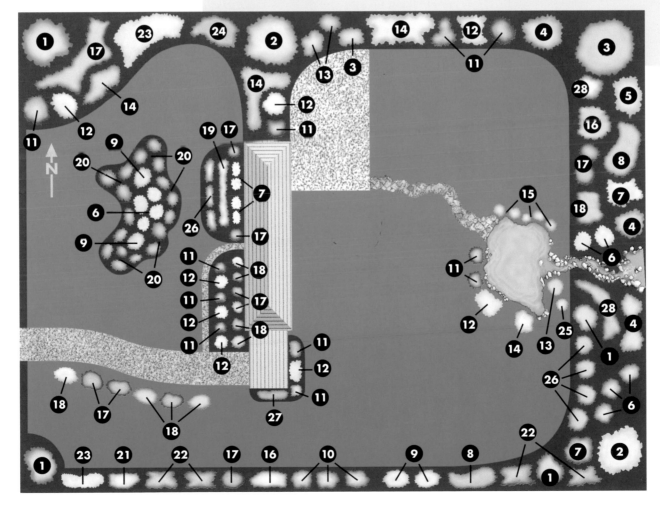

PACIFIC NORTHWEST
REGIONAL GARDEN

1. **Wild Plums and Cherries** (*Prunus* species)
2. **Willows** (*Salix* species)
3. **Aspens or Poplars** (*Populus* species)
4. **Wild Lilacs** (*Ceanothus* species)
5. **Buckthorns** (*Rhamnus* species)
6. **Nasturtium** (*Tropaeolium* species)
7. **Cabbage and Mustards** (*Brassica* species)
8. **Hollyhocks** (*Alcea rosea*)
9. **Sunflowers** (*Helianthus*) **and** ***Rudbeckia* species**
10. **Carrots** (*Daucus carota*), **Dill** (*Anethum graveolens*)
11. **Buddleia**
12. **Mints**
13. **Zinnias**

WHERE AND WHEN TO PLANT

The butterfly garden should be set up as early in the spring as weather conditions permit. Prepare the soil well with lots of organic material, such as peat moss, and a mild fertilizer, such as decomposed cow manure, and composted yard-waste materials, working these organic substances into the soil at least 12 inches (30cm) deep.

Allow the soil to sit a week and water it daily, letting the bacteria in the soil break down the organic matter into nutrients available for plant growth. Use this time to plan the final design and layout of your butterfly garden. You will want to try a variety of layouts to fit your available space. For example, try breaking up a square or rectangular lawn area with several "islands" or raised mounds of dirt, creating picturesque focal points for colorful flower displays that will attract butterflies much more readily than if all the flowers are at the same level or crowded into a border zone at the edges of a broad but attractively sterile green lawn area.

Have some planter areas in full sun, maybe in the center of your lawn, with other areas in shade or partial shade. This will not only allow you to use a wider variety of plants in your butterfly garden, but it will also attract a wider variety of butterflies that may prefer intermediate levels of solar radiation instead of full sun.

Look at some of the sample layouts that are presented in this book (pages 27-31)

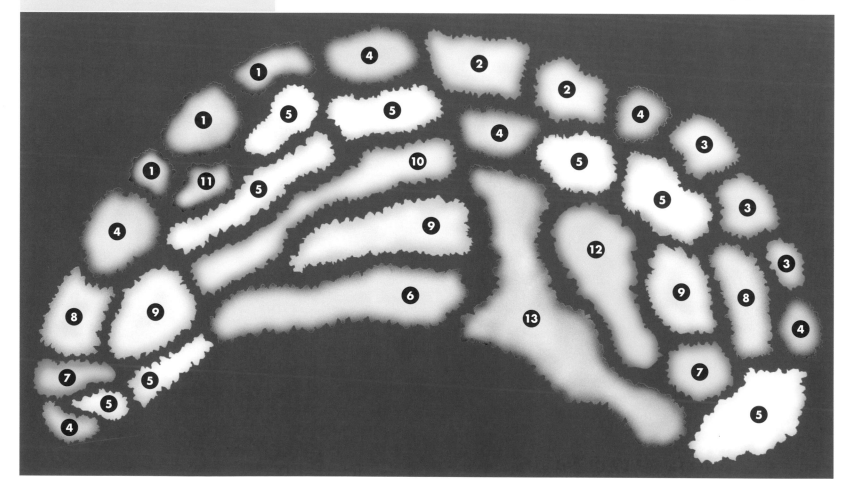

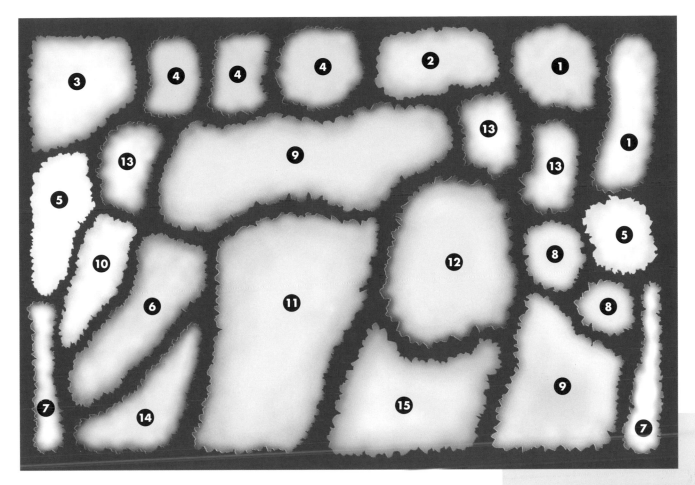

and at the photographs. Note that it is usually best to arrange your plants by relative heights. Start in the foreground with low-growing plants, such as sedum or prostrate verbena. Follow these with intermediate height plants, such as impatiens and heliotrope. Zinnias and marigolds make an effective intermediate height stand. Behind these, on the highest part of your raised "islands of dirt" or at the back of your border area, place your tallest-growing shrubs, such as milkweed, pentas, and buddleia. Even porterweed, if well-fertilized, may grow 4 to 5 feet (1.2 to 1.5m) tall and be placed at the back of your garden for most effective display.

Besides taking into consideration the physical size of your mature plants, consider varying the color. As much as possible, group six to ten plants together with the same color, and then alternate with another group of plants having a strongly contrasting color. Thus, a group of red pentas may effectively set off white mints next to them, with orange-flowered milkweeds behind the mints. A light purple- or white-flowered buddleia in the back can provide another striking contrast with a group of mixed flowering species in front. In planting impatiens, definitely use masses of eight to ten plants of a single color in one area, alternating with the next color. With impatiens, choose bright orange- or red-flowered plants for maximum attractiveness to butterflies such as Swallowtails and Sulphurs. Choose some white-flowered

SOUTHWEST
REGIONAL GARDEN

1. **Wild Plums and Cherries** (*Prunus* species)
2. **Willows** (*Salix* species)
3. **Aspens, Poplars, Cottonwoods with Mistletoes** (*Populus* tree species)
4. **Wild Lilacs** (*Ceanothus* species)
5. **Buckthorns** (*Rhamnus* species)
6. **Milkweed** (*Asclepias* species)
7. **Passionvines** (*Passiflora* species)
8. **Hollyhocks** (*Alcea rosea*)
9. **Pentas**
10. **Porterweed**
11. **Lantana**
12. **Verbena**
13. **Buddleia**
14. **Heliotrope**
15. **Mints**

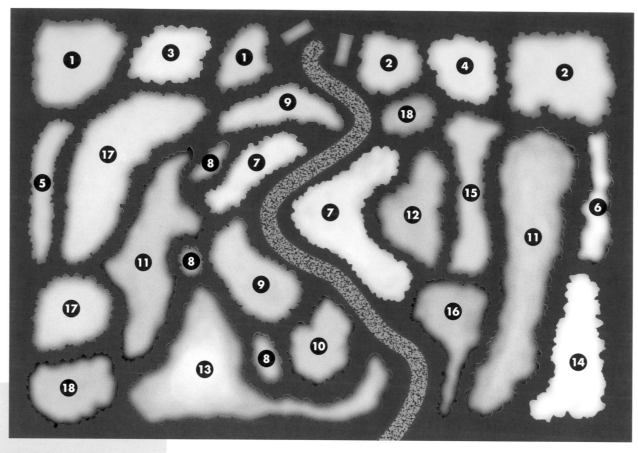

SOUTHEAST
REGIONAL GARDEN

1. **Wild Cherry** (*Prunus* species)
2. **Poplar** (*Populus* species)
3. **Spicebush** (*Lindera benzoin*)
4. **Sassafrass** (*Sassafrass albidum*)
5. **Pipevines** (*Aristolochia* species)
6. **Passionvines** (*Passiflora* species)
7. **Snapdragons** (*Antirrhinum* species)
8. **Canna lilies**
9. **Pentas** (*assorted colors*)
10. **Salvia** (*red or purple*)
11. **Impatiens**
12. **Milkweed** (*Asclepias* species)
13. **Aster** (*Asteraceae*)
14. **Wild Senna** (*Cassia* species)
15. **Dill** (*Ruta graveolens*)
16. **Verbena** (*Verbenaceae*)
17. **Lantana**
18. **Buddleia**

impatiens, however, to attract day-flying and evening-flying Sphinx moths to your butterfly garden.

You can sometimes get good ideas from seeing sale displays at your local plant center and nursery, looking at how they have arranged their plants for effective display to the buying public. Combinations that attract you may look equally attractive to butterflies in the garden. You can also get good ideas for garden layouts and plant species at your local botanical garden, especially in the butterfly garden section. Also, if you join any of the butterfly associations mentioned in chapter 4, you will get ideas for new plant species to try and new arrangements to consider from reading their publications. Many times, the members of these groups are active in

exchanging seeds and other plant propagules for mutual enhancement of butterfly gardens. They will include ads or announcements in their newsletters which offer free exchanges of varieties for species from your area, or sell plants at very low cost.

ATTRACTING A VARIETY
OF BUTTERFLY SPECIES

The greater the variety of plants that you have in the garden, including both nectar sources and larval host plants, the greater variety of butterfly species and number of butterflies you will attract. Thus, there is a definite benefit to planting a large garden with many different species, growing under different conditions of full sun, semishade, and full shade.

A second secret to increasing the variety of butterfly species in your garden is to plan for a series of seasonal changes in the flowering species present in your garden. In other words, seek out a variety of plants that will bloom in the spring, summer, and fall months, either in succession or continuously. Your local nurserymen can offer excellent advice on selecting plants to achieve this end. It usually works out best to mix the spring, summer, and fall blooming species in your garden's physical arrangement or layout so that the blooms of one species are complemented by the foliage background of another plant during its nonblooming season.

In addition to planting a variety of nectar sources and host plants, and seeking out plants that will bloom at different seasons, you can plan to provide places for butterflies to hide during rainstorms, or even sheltered areas for nighttime resting and winter hibernation. Some of the most familiar Nymphalid butterflies, such as Mourning Cloak, Anglewings, and Tortoiseshells, hibernate during the winter as adults inside hollow logs and stumps, or similar sheltered places. You can provide some of these sites in the garden, and plant vegetation around them to make them look like part of the natural landscape, just as in a forest meadow. When you plant passionflower vines to attract the Zebra Heliconian (or even the Julia butterfly in south Florida), put some in a shaded area with lots of twiggy-branched trees around them (if you have the space and opportunity). You will be pleasantly surprised some day to see a roost of Zebra butterflies gathering on these dead branches in the late

CENTRAL AND NORTHEAST
REGIONAL GARDEN

1. **Willows** (*Salix* species)
2. **Plums and Cherries** (*Prunus* species)
3. **Poplars** (*Populus* species)
4. **Wild Senna** (*Cassia* species)
5. **Asters** (Asteraceae)
6. **Verbena** (Verbenaceae)
7. **Buddleia**
8. **Heliotrope**
9. **Milkweed** (*Asclepias* species)
10. **Mints**
11. **Snapdragons** (*Antirrhinum* species)
12. **Spicebush** (*Lindera benzoin*)
13. **Sassafrass** (*Sassafrass albidum*)
14. **Violets** (*Viola* species)
15. **Fennel** (*Foeniculum vulgare*)
16. **Pipevines** (*Aristoiochia* species)
17. **Zinnias**

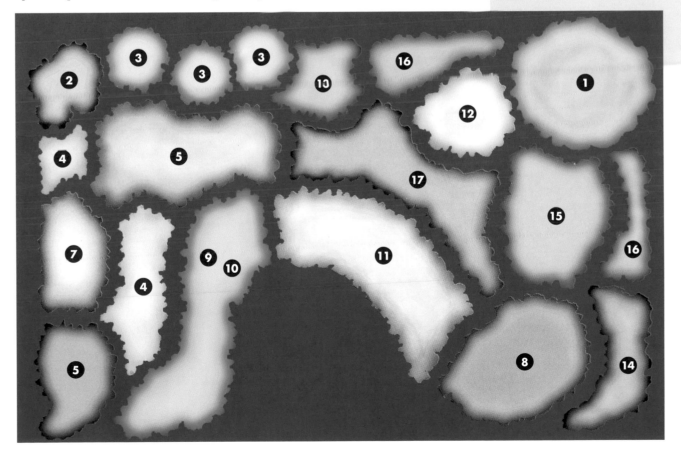

afternoon, flying very slowly around the branches and packing themselves by the dozens along each branch until a thick social congregation has gathered for the night. If they like this spot and are protected from any disturbance there, they will return to the branch night after night for months on end, forming this nightly social roost.

A well-chosen selection of large-leaf shrubs and trees around your garden will provide sheltered places for butterflies to hide during inclement weather and to spend the night. In addition, the variety of shade and sunlight that these large plants provide will make the widest possible variety of butterflies feel at home in your butterfly garden.

PROVIDING WATER: STREAMS, PONDS AND WATERFALLS

If you have a particularly creative bent, or are talented in landscaping, you may want to provide a source of water in your garden in the form of a small stream, a fish pond, and a waterfall cascading into the stream or pond. Not only will the sound and sight of rushing water make your garden a more pleasant area for you, it will also attract an amazing number of butterflies! Butterflies need water on hot days and often visit moist sand or moist rocks to drink water for minutes at a time. If you provide a small waterfall, stream, and/or pond, Swallowtails will fly around that area and may land and line up along the edge to drink. Aggregations of Sulphur butterflies will gather at noontime to imbibe water and dissolved salts, and many a Nymphalid, Blue, and even Hairstreak will fly down to drink, along with Skippers and other species. You will find many species that normally are rather shy will allow you to approach within inches of them as they drink for many minutes, totally absorbed in

**Top: Asters (*Aster novae-angliae* 'Hella Lacy')
mixed with *Miscanthus sinensis* make very
effective mass displays.
Bottom left: The Painted Lady butterfly (*Vanessa
cardui*) alights on a purple coneflower to drink
nectar. This renowned migrant species moves
north in great numbers during the springtime
and southward in less obvious migrations
during the fall months.
Bottom right: Among these yarrow (*Achillea*)
plants in the garden has been placed a
"butterfly house," with slits in the front to allow
Nymphalid butterflies such as Anglewings and
Mourning Cloaks to enter in the fall and
hibernate over the winter months.**

A beautiful garden scene in Niche Gardens, at Chapel Hill, North Carolina, shows how rocks and water can be used with plants in a small space.

the refreshing treat of drinking water that is surprisingly hard to find in an urban setting on a hot summer day.

ROCKY CRAGS AND FRUIT TREES: ADDING STRUCTURES FOR SPECIAL SPECIES

If your backyard is built into a hillside, or you have the opportunity to haul large rocks into part of your garden and build a rocky crag or cliff, you can plant rock plants such as Sedum species or other host plants of Parnassius butterflies (if you live in a mountain area in the West), or other special rock-garden plants that will be attractive to your local butterflies. A beautiful rock garden can be just as attractive to butterflies and moths as a flatland garden. Try planting phlox, daisies, fleabane and other asters, and even alpine sunflowers, to attract butterflies to nectar and to potential use of the plants as larval hosts.

You may also wish to try some fruit or shade trees in your garden. For example, the tulip tree (*Liriodendron* species) is a favorite host plant for the Eastern Tiger Swallowtail, and is a magnificent shade tree in its own right. Male Swallowtails may "hilltop" around the tops of such large trees in your garden, a phenomenon where males congregate and seek females at the highest point in the surrounding area. This could be your tree if you plan accordingly. Fruit trees, such as wild cherries, are attractive host plants as well, not only to some butterflies but also to moths. You can study our list of larval host plants in the identification table (page 23) to determine some of the best trees to use.

With continued work on your butterfly garden project, and by reading the literature and visiting other gardens and nursery displays, you will soon discover a great many additional features that you may wish to add to your plans for the butterfly garden. The suggestions in this section are to get you started and to show you how quickly the butterflies will find even the simplest garden, rewarding you faster than you probably thought possible!

CHAPTER THREE

Maintaining Your Butterfly Garden

I n many ways, a butterfly garden is like any other garden. Butterfly gardens require a minimal amount of care in watering, fertilizing, and controlling pests such as weeds (nondesirable plants) and insects or nematodes, fungi, and other organisms that attack the plants you want to save for the butterflies. Sometimes butterfly gardens are hit by unexpected nontarget spraying, such as spraying by the city for mosquito control and herbicide spraying along the roadside adjacent to your property, or similar unexpected disasters. This chapter covers the most important points of maintaining the butterfly garden at its best in the face of all these needs and concerns.

The common passionflower species of the South, *Passiflora incarnata*, is probably the most widely cultivated garden passionflower and is extremely attractive to the Gulf Fritillary. The Gulf Fritillary larvae will soon decimate your vine unless you have an extensive trellis and plant a number of vines to support the large butterfly population that will gather to eat the plants.

A butterfly garden can be allowed to "naturalize" by carefully selecting plants initially and then allowing their free growth and natural re-seeding annually, as in this garden in Wisconsin.

WATERING

If you are landscaping with native plants, especially those found in your immediate geographic area, then you normally have little to worry about as regards watering, for local plants are well adapted to the climatic factors prevalent in your area. However, we do not always have that luxury of independence from watering. An unusual drought or cold spell may affect your plants and those of the surrounding countryside, and, if you are not watching the situation, you may lose many or all of your treasured plants to wilting or freezing. When landscaping with native plants, it is best to be prepared to water occasionally via a sprinkler system or hand-held hose, in the event that natural rainfall patterns are atypically absent or delayed. Having a watering system in place

can also save you on an unexpectedly cold night in the fall, when damage from a hard freeze can be avoided by coating your plants with water before the temperature drops to freezing and allowing ice to form on them, maintaining a temperature of 32°F (0°C) on the plants while the surrounding air temperature drops lower at night. This, of course, will keep your garden green for only a few additional days or perhaps several weeks, but the butterflies will appreciate your valiant efforts in your use of water as an antifreeze damage measure.

For ordinary watering, especially of non-native plants such as various species of passionflowers or pipevines that may not normally be found in your area of the country, it is best to water every day in hot weather, or every second or third day in mild

weather. Long, well-spaced soakings are better than short, light, frequent soakings that might not penetrate the soil very far. It is usually easier on your schedule as well to do thorough soakings at greater intervals.

One special concern in watering may be the water temperature and quality. Normally, the water provided by the city's water mains or by your well flows out at a low temperature that is not injurious to the plants and their root systems. However, if you have allowed your hose to sit out in the open, and it is backed up with water behind a closed sprinkler head, you may want to spray the water on a rock wall or bare ground for a couple of minutes to allow the cooler water to reach the nozzle before spraying your plants. Otherwise, you can parboil your prize impatiens or other flower displays in short order with overheated hose water! If you are using well water with a high sulfur or iron content, you will notice a strong odor while watering. This does not affect your butterflies (or, normally, the plants) and in fact may actually prove attractive to some butterfly species.

FERTILIZING

With native plants, grown in soils typical of your area, there is little or no need to fertilize after initial establishment of the plant. You may use a hormone powder, such as Roottone, on the stems of cuttings to encourage early root growth. Otherwise, a high-powered fertilizer is not only unnecessary but probably injurious to most native species. However, if you are using nectar sources like

impatiens, pentas, or even buddleia and other similar introduced plants, including larval food plants such as exotic (non-native) passionflower and pipevine, you will definitely want to use fertilizers to enhance growth and make your garden look its best during all of the growing season in your area. You can establish a fertilization regime in three ways.

First, when you prepare your garden bed in spring for planting annuals and new perennials, you will find it advantageous to spread an inch (2.5cm) or so of decomposed cow manure or several inches of organic compost across the soil surface, and then work it in with a pitchfork or shovel to a depth of 12 inches (30cm) or so. When you plant your seedlings and potted plants from the nursery in a well-prepared soil like this, it

is amazing how fast they will take root and how well they will grow.

After four weeks or so, following the establishment phase, you will want to begin regular fertilization with a higher-powered-fertilizer. We find that Osmokote, a slow-release fertilizer in pellet form, is especially good with the great majority of perennials and annuals that we grow in our butterfly garden. The pellets slowly release fertilizer for the next three to six months in quantities that seem perfect for most plants to absorb and utilize immediately. The pellet fertilizers of this type are relatively expensive in initial outlay for a bag, but then it only takes one application per season to insure that your garden grows to its finest degree through the summer and fall months.

Alternatively, if you prefer to apply less concentrated granular fertilizers, such as 6-6-6, or liquid fertilizers, such as Peter's Formula 20-20-20, which are used up quickly in the soil after application, you can apply these every two weeks or so around the bases of the stems of each plant and get excellent results. With a little care and regular fertilization like this, it is amazing how healthy your garden will look all spring, summer, and fall, and how most of your plants will bloom continuously, making it a verdant paradise for every butterfly in the neighborhood.

PEST CONTROL
IN THE BUTTERFLY GARDEN

As you can imagine, if you are creating perfect conditions for plant growth and blooming, your garden will attract not only butterflies but many pest species, which may attack both your luxuriant plant growth and the butterflies that form part of their own natural diet. Thus, you will probably need to

A wall of nasturtium can be achieved very easily by providing some support for the plants to climb on. The well-fertilized nasturtiums shown here have grown far better than the usual low growth of the flowers, often used as border plantings.

combat pest infestations to make your butterfly garden a reasonably safe environment for all the butterflies you are attracting from the surrounding area or growing on your larval hosts and to keep the garden looking its best.

First, let's consider the common problem of superabundant plant pests such as aphids, mealybugs, whiteflies, and stink bugs. The luxuriant plant growth produced by your regular watering and fertilizing will make your garden a perfect habitat for any herbivorous insect that likes those plants. If you spray a pyrethrin or organophosphate insecticide on your plants, you are liable to kill the butterfly caterpillars that you want to grow there. Likewise, if you use a systemic insecticide that is absorbed into the plant and carried by its circulatory system throughout every stem and leaf to poison an herbivorous pest, you may also give the butterfly visitor a lethal dose of insecticide in the nectar that it imbibes from the flower head. Thus with many sucking insects and related pests of your garden's plants, it is probably best to retreat to the tried-and-true methods of a simpler time, before synthetic chemical pesticides were widely adopted.

You can make a very good bug spray for injurious insects and mildew with a mild detergent soap solution, using several tablespoons of dishwashing detergent per gallon of warm water. Put this in a hand sprayer and spray it directly on the fungi, sucking insect pests, or predacious plant bugs. This will reduce the infestation to manageable or negligible levels. You can also use a mild nicotine spray, obtainable at your local nursery, and spray this as a contact poison. You can dust sulfur powder on these plants and achieve the same result. All of these treatments will easily wash off with the next rain or watering cycle, so you may have to

Lantana camara may be the single most effective butterfly flower in North America. The best varieties to obtain are lower mound-forming types, like this 'Yellow Sage' variety, photographed at Old Westbury Gardens in Old Westbury, New York.

treat the garden several times to achieve the desired results. In the meantime, your butterflies, at least, will still be safe from harm.

Sometimes pests of other types appear, such as large webs made by orb-weaving spiders, lizards, or insectivorous birds that may be looking for a butterfly meal in your butterfly garden. There is little you can do about these pests; in fact, they are part of the natural order of things in the garden community. It is a good idea to leave these birds, lizards, and even praying mantises alone because although they capture a few butterflies, they are also feeding on many injurious plant pests that you may not want in your garden, such as cutworm moths, plant bugs, or army worm moth larvae. Indeed, part of the fascination of a butterfly garden is watching the endlessly varied interplay of natural ecological forces at work right outside your window. Watching a mockingbird or Carolina wren capture a caterpillar and take the prey to its nest to feed its newly hatched young is part of the fascination of nature for children and adults alike and provides invaluable lessons about the interrelatedness of all organisms. Since part of your aim in creating a butterfly garden is to preserve a little bit of the natural world in your own yard, just enjoy these interactions and be thankful that you have such a favored place for all these creatures to interact.

PROTECTING YOUR BUTTERFLIES AGAINST NONTARGET SPRAYING

In many areas of the country, the local city or county authorities regularly spray fogs of pesticides around home and business properties (at least the front yards) from trucks. These sprays are usually applied for adult mosquito control, but may also be applied for various pest insects such as the Gypsy Moth. Occasionally, a mosquito control district or forestry office may use airplanes or helicopters for aerial spraying of various pesticides. Most authorities will respond to a phone call requesting that your property not be sprayed due to sensitive organisms being there, such as fish in an outdoor fish pond (which make an excellent addition to your butterfly garden anyway), pets such as cats or dogs or tropical birds, or sensitive children with allergies. Occasionally, though, a public health emergency may be declared (as for mosquitoes that could potentially spread encephalitis) or an agricultural quarantine emergency may be imposed on the area (such as for the Mediterranean fruit fly or Caribbean fruit fly in southern California or southern Florida metropolitan areas), and you have little choice but to hope that most of your butterfly friends have gotten under cover of leaves and will stay quiet until the spraying has passed. You can turn on your sprinklers and water the garden after such generalized nontarget spraying, too, in order to wash the chemical residues off the flowers and leaves as soon as possible.

The same general problem occurs when roadsides are sprayed with herbicides to reduce weed growth or when railroad tracks and utility power line right-of-ways are sprayed to eliminate plant growth. An unexpected drift of spray on a light wind can come onto your property and kill nontarget insects such as the butterflies flying around your garden. Many butterfly enthusiasts have found that if they organize public opinion in their community, they can bring the responsible authorities around to the point of view that natural wildflower growth along roadsides, railroad right-of-ways, and power lines is an attractive, positive feature of the environment, and one that should be cherished, not eliminated. Enlist the aid of your local garden clubs, service clubs, and, of course, your local newspaper editors in such drives, and you will be surprised at how successful you can be in eliminating unnecessary herbicide spraying and unnecessary pesticide spraying for mosquito control or forest pest insects such as the Gypsy Moth. Again, with herbicides as with mosquito spraying drift, you can best remove the spray residues by promptly watering your garden and washing the flowers and leaves after any drift of spray onto your property.

CARING FOR YOUR BUTTERFLY GARDEN

At first glance, it might seem a difficult task to maintain your butterfly garden in the face of various natural and human-generated disturbances or threats. But with a little organization of your daily and weekly schedule, your watering, fertilizing, and pest control will soon become simply additional enjoyable times that you spend in your garden. Many times while watering, you will have the opportunity to observe butterflies close up and see their reactions to each other and to other animals that pass through your garden. This is often the best time to see butterflies laying eggs or doing other interesting things that you would not normally have the chance to observe. So make the best of the time spent in your garden, and treasure every moment.

CHAPTER FOUR
Enjoying Your Butterfly Garden

s butterflies appear more and more frequently in your garden and the diversity changes with the seasons, you will notice some butterflies staying and making their homes among your plants. They will mate and lay their eggs on your host plants and soon caterpillars will be growing up and pupating, readying the next generation of residents. Other species will come in from time to time as visitors, staying awhile and then flitting on to parts unknown. Some of these will be migrants, heading northward through your area in the spring and southward in the fall. All have their interesting stories to tell. If you are able to identify the species you see, you will be able to learn much more about them, including their life

The Western Tiger Swallowtail (*Papilio rutulus*) is potentially one of the most regular visitors to a butterfly garden in the western United States during the spring and summer months. Males are territorial, live a long time, and fly the same route through the neighborhood daily.

histories and their behavioral habits, from the many books available on North American butterflies.

IDENTIFYING YOUR BUTTERFLY VISITORS AND RESIDENTS

The first step to identifying your visiting and resident butterflies is to thumb through the gallery of butterflies shown in the photographs in chapter 6. We have selected the best color illustrations of the most frequent visitors to butterfly gardens across North America and have included some basic information about their range and life history stages, as well as preferred nectar plants for the adults and host plants for the larvae.

If you do not find a particular butterfly in the illustrations, you can usually determine a close relative of it from the pictures, and then use the scientific name to do a little detective work in field guides or major identification manuals for the North American butterfly fauna. For example, if you find a large, pale white Swallowtail with black stripes landing on wild lilac in your California garden, and the closest butterfly you can find to it is the Western Tiger Swallowtail, *Papilio rutulus*, you can use the first (genus) name of the two-part scientific name and look it up in the index of a butterfly manual obtained at your local library or bookstore. Once you find the section on *Papilio* species in a book, you can look through the pictures until you find this black-striped, pale species, which turns out to be the Pale Swallowtail, *Papilio eurymedon*. Then you will discover what its food plants are and can add these to your garden!

There are many excellent butterfly manuals available today which you can buy from your favorite bookstore or borrow from the local public or school library. *National Audubon Society Field Guide to North*

American Butterflies by Robert Michael Pyle (Alfred A. Knopf, 1981) is an excellent pocket-size guide that has color photographs of both the upper side and under side of most of the North American butterfly species. James A. Scott's book, *The Butterflies of North America* (Stanford University Press, 1986) also covers the North American fauna, using color plates of specimens arranged or grouped by their general color patterns for ease of identification. *The Butterflies of North America* (Doubleday, 1975), edited by William H. Howe, is also a very inclusive manual that has excellent color plates of all the North American species. Alexander B. Klots's *A Field Guide to the Butterflies of North America, East of the Great Plains* (Houghton Mifflin, 1951) is an older field guide available in most libraries, and it has recently been revised completely by Paul A. Opler for a new edition with excellent color plates. For the western butterflies, one can use J. W. Tilden and Arthur Smith's, *A Field Guide to Western Butterflies* (Houghton Mifflin, 1985).

There are also a great many books that deal with butterflies of specific states, or parts of states, and oftentimes, these are the most satisfactory for local use because they include only the species that would be expected to occur in your area. Thus in southern California, one might want to use Thomas C. Emmel and John F. Emmel's, *The Butterflies of Southern California* (Natural History Museum of Los Angeles County, 1973). Around Seattle, Washington, one would want to find and use a copy of Robert Michael Pyle's *Watching Washington Butterflies* (The Mountaineers, 1974). Across Missouri, a copy of *Butterflies and Moths of Missouri* by Richard Heitzman and Roger Heitzman (Missouri Highway Commission, 1987) would be highly useful. In southern Florida, *Butterflies of the Florida Keys* by Marc C. Minno and Thomas C. Emmel (Scientific Publishers, 1993) is an invaluable manual for the 106 species recorded in south Florida and the Florida Keys. You can refer to the boxed guide on

The full-grown larva of the Pale Swallowtail (*Papilio eurymedon*) feeds on *Rhamnus* and looks like a small snake when approached from the front. The eyespots on the thorax here are completely "fake"; the true eyes are located on the front of the head and are tiny round bumps.

page 47 to find other published state and local books.

If you are fortunate enough to see a butterfly that can't be matched to any illustration in one of these books, you may have found either an aberration (the result of an environmentally caused alteration of the development of the wing pattern), or a true genetic mutation, which has greatly altered the wing pattern from its normal appearance. Alternatively, you may have found a rare migrant or stray specimen of a species that normally does not occur in your area. These special specimens are usually best identified by taking photographs of them to an expert at your local museum, university, or college and seeing if they can help you identify the specimen. Since you probably will not be collecting the visitor and resident butterflies in your garden, a photograph is the next best thing to the actual specimen for such identification. In the next section, we talk about the ways to photograph butterflies, both for a permanent record of each species that visits your garden and for enjoyment as another facet of butterfly gardening.

PHOTOGRAPHING BUTTERFLIES

You can photograph butterflies with almost any camera, even an Instamatic type that doesn't require focusing or careful distance measurements. You will need a reasonably fast film that allows you to take pictures in either sunlight or shade, depending on where your butterfly is sitting or hovering at the moment you snap its picture. Otherwise, you can point and shoot and achieve basically good results, as regards a record of the butterfly's general appearance.

But to really record the delicate scales, colorful patterns, and intricate behavior of these relatively small creatures, you may wish to consider investing in a 35mm camera with a macro lens, allowing you to focus as close as 2 inches (5cm) or so from the butterfly. Some of the many satisfactory cameras of this type include Nikon, Pentax, Minolta, Olympus, and other similar models. You can buy these models with many automatic features that will even focus the camera and determine the right lens setting to use, or you can get a simple manual camera, with a macro focusing lens, often at a reasonable price in the used equipment section of your camera shop. The macro lens will allow you not only to take close-up pictures of the butterflies, but also wider-angle shots of the most attractive parts of your butterfly garden through the year. If you are taking many close-up shots, you may wish to invest in an electronic flash unit that will illuminate your butterfly object even under the dimmest conditions of shady woods or cloudy days. By using a flash, you can also use the smallest possible diaphragm opening on your camera lens, allowing the maximum depth of field (focus range) in your pictures.

The choice of film in your camera is up to you. Many people like to make prints to put in an album or to place on the wall in the form of spectacular enlargements. In those cases, choosing a good color print film (a negative film like Kodacolor) is the best choice. Others, especially teachers and people planning to give lectures to garden clubs or other groups, may wish to choose a positive transparency film (like Kodachrome, Ektachrome, or Fujichrome) so that they can make 35mm slides and project them. Such slides can also be used for making quite satisfactory color prints and enlargements.

With the new color scanners available now for computers, it is possible to take a slide or a print and make inexpensive recordings in full color on your hard drive which can be used later to print out photos in newsletters, journals, or even enlarged color prints of the butterflies for the enjoyment for you and your friends.

Many people, intrigued by the nearly constant motion and beautiful flight patterns of butterflies, especially in their courtship behavior, but even in nectaring, find that using a video camera with a macro-zoom lens is a wonderful way to record living butterflies in the garden. Many good cameras available now have push-button controls, making it very easy to follow a butterfly around the garden and take wide scenic shots as well as extreme close-ups. If one makes a mistake on the videotape, it is easy to reverse it and record over it again in the next few minutes. With the proper editing equipment, you can assemble a wonderful series of tapes on the different species that come to your garden, their life histories, their behavior, and even unusual events like predators grabbing a butterfly or a parasite laying its eggs under a caterpillar's skin. Anyone interested in this phase of photography in the butterfly garden ought to acquire a copy of the National Audubon Society's *Butterflies for Beginners*, a one-hour videotape that includes close-up looks at thirty-two of the most common and wide-ranging North American butterflies. The tape is available from MasterVision, 969 Park Avenue, New York, New York 10028. Dr. Paul A. Opler and Jim Ebner, the experts who prepared this videotape, include the entire life cycle of each of the butterflies in their tape and describe the adults' distinguishing features and interesting behaviors.

RECORDING YOUR OBSERVATIONS

One of the fun things to do with your butterfly garden on the very first day is to start a list of the species that you see coming to the garden. This can start as a simple list of species names, and by adding to it each day, you can make a "life list" of the butterflies you see over the years. You will soon note that some species occur only rarely, or may appear one year and not another. Likewise, some species occur early in the spring, while others appear in midsummer, and still others may not fly in your area until the fall months. You might even wish to develop a simple chart, with the species names on the vertical axis and the months and days of the year on the horizontal axis, and put a check for each species on each day you observe it in your garden. This will help you to see seasonal patterns and perhaps even to prepare the garden better for those visitors by being aware of the need to plant their favorite flowers in time for their emergence next year. You may discover, for example, that in your area of the country, the Cloudless Giant Sulphur (*Phoebis sennae*), arrives in May, flying northward on its migration, and that it heads south in September and October. Planting red pentas in time for these butterflies will attract countless numbers to your garden during their two annual migrations. By developing and keeping such charts, many butterfly gardeners have learned some very interesting facts about territorial behavior of Red Admiral butterflies appearing at the same time of the year in their yards, or seasonal emergences of successive broods of certain species in their areas.

You can also keep a daily journal, obser-ving your butterflies and recording your observations in narrative form. What did the butterflies visit most that day? What interesting behaviors did you see? Did the butterflies start laying eggs this year in April, or did they wait until May as usual, even though you had a very warm and early spring in your area? Are any of the caterpillars of certain species showing up on food plants in your garden which you had not previously seen them on? There are now a number of butterfly gardening newsletters which would be very pleased to receive your submission of notes of your observations and publish them. Likewise, if you develop a really pleasing butterfly garden layout and have unusual success with attracting butterflies, you may wish to write a magazine article for one of the many gardening magazines or butterfly enthusiast journals, such as *American Butterflies* (published by the North American Butterfly Association), *News of the Lepidopterists' Society* (published by the Lepidopterists' Society), *Southern Living*, *Sunset Magazine*, and other regional magazines catering to the general gardening public and horticultural trade.

The Cloudless Giant Sulphur occurs across the southern half of the United States and strays as far north as the Canadian border during the summer. Lantana, buddleia, salvia, and other flowers can readily attract it to your garden.

If you are also a photographer, you can use your own pictures to illustrate your journal or articles that you write for publication.

If you do not have photographic skills yourself, you may wish to involve a friend who is a particularly enthusiastic camera bug and get him or her to help you in this endeavor. You can even do ink sketches to include with your articles. You will find that sharing your enthusiasm and knowledge of butterflies, whether with a single friend or thousands of readers, will greatly enhance your own enjoyment of your garden, as well as their lives.

CONTACT WITH OTHER ENTHUSIASTS

As you expand your knowledge of butterflies and of butterfly gardening, you will probably find it very helpful and stimulating to get in contact with other enthusiasts on a regular basis. There are many organizations that publish newsletters, journals, and magazines which regularly contain articles on butterfly gardening or on identifying the colorful species that show up in your garden. You may also want to travel to some of the major public butterfly gardens in the United States and abroad to get inspired by their designs, purchase new butterfly nectar plants and caterpillar host plants, or just experience the ambiance of total immersion in a well-landscaped display containing thousands of American and foreign butterflies. This section will help you with those contacts.

Butterfly Associations

Following are some of the organizations that you can join to learn more about butterfly gardening and butterflies in general and to receive publications on a regular basis.

The North American Butterfly Association, Inc.
4 Delaware Road
Morristown, New Jersey 07960

This organization was formed to educate the public about the joys of nonconsumptive, recreational butterfly activities, including gar-dening, listing species, observation, photography, rearing, and conservation. Membership in NABA is open to everyone who shares those interests. Members receive a beautiful quarterly journal, *American Butterflies*, which has been published since 1993. Full-color articles cover the ins and outs of butterfly gardening. This is probably the best general organization for the beginner; it covers all of North America and publishes articles of wide popular interest.

The Lepidopterists' Society
c/o Los Angeles County Museum of
Natural History
900 Exposition Boulevard
Los Angeles, California 90007-4057

The Lepidopterists' Society has been in existence for more than fifty years, and it publishes two regular periodicals: *The News of the Lepidopterists' Society*, a bimonthly or quarterly newsletter containing many articles of general interest, and the *Journal of the Lepidopterists' Society*, a more technical quarterly publication with papers of interest to advanced students of butterflies.

The Xerces Society
10 S.W. Ash Street
Portland, Oregon 97204

This international nonprofit organization is dedicated to insects and other invertebrates, and the preservation of critical biosystems worldwide. They publish a quarterly magazine called *Wings: Essays on Invertebrate Conservation,* which occasionally contains articles on butterfly gardening.

Association for Tropical Lepidoptera
P. O. Box 141210
Gainesville, Florida 32614-1210

The Association for Tropical Lepidoptera is a nonprofit organization for the support of research on the biology, systematics, and conservation of tropical, subtropical, and temperate Lepidoptera of the world. It publishes two journals, *Holarctic Lepidoptera*, which covers butterflies and moths of North America, Europe, and northern Asia, and *Tropical Lepidoptera*, which covers the subtropical and tropical areas of the world. Each journal comes out twice a year, and is filled with hundreds of pages of colorful articles on butterflies and moths. The *Tropical Lepidoptera News* is a newsletter that comes out quarterly and contains additional articles of interest to butterfly enthusiasts, including book reviews, field trip descriptions, and stories about famous lepidopterists.

Travel for Butterflying

The best ideas often come not from books but from personal experience. As you get more interested in butterflies and butterfly gardening, you may want to travel to get inspiration from other butterfly gardeners and butterfly displays, and even go on your own or with groups of people to other areas of North America and abroad.

A good place to start your travel for butterflying is with a trip to the nearest large botanical garden. Many of these gardens now have butterfly garden areas where you can see how expert horticulturists lay out and display flowering plants to attract butterflies. (Unfortunately, most botanical gardens plant only butterfly nectar sources and not caterpillar food plants as well, but hopefully that will change in the future.) Large and elaborate gardens such as the Santa Ana Botanical Garden in southern California and the Missouri Botanical Garden in St. Louis have many experts on their staff who may be able to answer some of your questions if you are having problems with particular plants or want to grow an unusual species in your area. They often have publications on how to start native plant gardens at home and how to design and plant butterfly gardens in your particular climatic zone, and other free or low-cost aids and advice.

Then you might want to consider a trip to one of the major United States butterfly gardens and display centers, such as Butterfly World at Coconut Creek, Florida; the Day Butterfly Center at Callaway Gardens in eastern Georgia; Wings of Wonder at Cypress Gardens, Florida; or the newer ones in Houston, Denver, Philadelphia, San Francisco, Tampa, and Niagara Falls. There you will be inspired by what full-time work on a butterfly garden can achieve. Just remember, though, that most of these enclosed displays and gardens purchase large numbers of pupae each week from suppliers who farm the butterfly species elsewhere in the world. You are keeping your open-air butterfly garden for native species, and so you ought to look particularly for hints and suggestions on how to cultivate plants and butterfly species native to your area, in other words, to obtain practical knowledge that you can apply readily to your home butterfly garden.

Some organizations such as the North American Butterfly Association (NABA) and many local butterfly societies (whose names and contact phone numbers you can learn through your local museum or university) have field trips to favored butterfly haunts, where in the company of like-minded amateurs and professionals, you can see a wonderful array of local species at the best time of the year and in the best location. Sometimes travel agencies offer special trips

A large-leafed *Solanum quitoense* from Ecuador is mixed with abundant flowers of *Lantana camara* and other wildflowers at Montrose Garden in Hillsborough, North Carolina.

to many parts of the world for butterfly watchers and butterfly collectors. You can join one of these trips and take your camera, net, or notebook along, and have a tremendously enjoyable time, learning from the others on the trip and the expert leaders. The leading agency in the United States offering such tours for butterfly enthusiasts is Expedition Travel, Inc. (1717 N.W. 45th Avenue, Gainesville, Florida 32605). Some of these trips include visits to the major butterfly gardens and displays in the world outside the United States, such as Penang Island and Kuala Lumpur in Malaysia, and the Taipei Zoo in Taiwan. You may also choose to visit natural sites with incredibly high

species diversity for butterflies. Among these are the Amazonian rain forest in central Rondonia, Brazil, where up to 1,800 species can live in a square mile. Or you can travel to Kenya's Kakamega Forest Reserve, where tens of thousands of individual butterflies swarm along the trails and roads through the equatorial rain forest.

As you can see, butterfly gardening can lead to a whole world of new adventures, filling your life with new and exciting experiences. Indeed, butterfly gardening can become a never-to-be-forgotten adventure in so many ways that you will wonder what you ever did before you discovered butterflies and butterfly gardening!

REGIONAL BUTTERFLY BOOKS FOR THE UNITED STATES AND CANADA

The following table lists some of the butterfly books currently available for particular geographic regions of the United States and Canada. You can usually find these at your local bookstore, university book shop, or public library. If there is a natural history museum in your area, you may be able to peruse or purchase copies of these books at its book store or library.

ARIZONA
Butterflies of Southeastern Arizona, by Richard A. Bailowitz and James P. Brock (Sonoran Arthropod Studies, Inc., Tucson, Arizona, 1991).

Butterflies of Grand Canyon National Park, by John S. Garth (Grand Canyon Natural History Association, Grand Canyon, Arizona, 1950).

CALIFORNIA
The Butterflies of Southern California, by Thomas C. Emmel and John F. Emmel (Natural History Museum of Los Angeles County, Los Angeles, 1973).

California Butterflies, by John S. Garth and J. W. Tilden (University of California Press, Berkeley, 1986).

The Butterflies of Orange County, California, by Larry J. Orsak (Museum of Systematic Biology, University of California, Irvine, 1978).

Butterflies of California, by John Adams Comstock (Reprint Edition: Introduction, Biography, and Revised Checklist by Thomas C. Emmel and John F. Emmel) (Scientific Publishers, Gainesville, FL, 1989).

CANADA
The Butterflies of Manitoba, by P. Klassen, A. R. Westwood, W. B. Preston, and W. B. McKillop (Manitoba Museum of Man and Nature, Winnipeg, 1989).

The Butterflies of Alberta, by John Acorn (Lone Pine Publishing, Edmonton, Alberta, 1993).

COLORADO
Colorado Butterflies, by F. M. Brown, D. F. Eff, and B. Rotger (Denver Museum of Natural History, Denver, 1957).

Florissant Butterflies: A Guide to the Fossil and Present-Day Species of Central Colorado, by T. C. Emmel, Marc C. Minno, and Boyce A. Drummond (Stanford University Press, Stanford, California, 1992).

EASTERN UNITED STATES
A Field Guide to the Butterflies of North America, East of the Great Plains, by Alexander B. Klots (Houghton Mifflin Company, Boston, Mass., 1951).

Butterflies East of the Great Plains, by Paul A. Opler and George O. Krizek (Johns Hopkins University Press, Baltimore, Maryland, 1984):

FLORIDA
Florida Butterflies, by Eugene J. Gerberg and Ross H. Arnett, Jr. (Natural Science Publications, Baltimore, Maryland, 1989).

Butterflies of the Florida Keys, by Marc C. Minno and Thomas C. Emmel (Scientific Publishers, Gainesville, FL, 1993).

Florida's Fabulous Butterflies, by Thomas C. Emmel (World Publications, Tampa, Florida, 1997).

GEORGIA
Butterflies of Georgia, by Lucien Harris, Jr. (University of Oklahoma Press, Norman, 1972).

ILLINOIS
The Butterflies of West-Central Illinois, by Yale Sedman and David F. Hess (Western Illinois University, Series in the Biological Sciences No. 11, 1985).

INDIANA
The Butterflies of Indiana, by Ernest M. Shull (Indiana University Press, Bloomington, 1987).

KANSAS
An Annotated List of the Butterflies of Kansas, by Charles A. Ely, Marvin D. Schwilling, and Marvin E. Rolls (Fort Hays State University, Museum of the High Plains, Hays, Kansas, 1986).

MINNESOTA
Butterflies, by Ralph W. Macy and Harold S. Shepard (University of Minnesota, 1941).

MISSOURI
Butterflies and Moths of Missouri, by J. Richard Heitzman and Joan E. Heitzman (Missouri Department of Conservation, Jefferson City, MO, 1987).

NORTH DAKOTA
Butterflies of North Dakota: An Atlas and Guide, by Ronald Allen Royer (Minot State University, Minot, ND, 1988).

OREGON
The Butterflies of Oregon, by Ernst J. Dornfeld (Timber Press, Forest Grove, Oregon, 1980).

PACIFIC NORTHWEST
Butterflies Afield in the Pacific Northwest, by W. A. Neill and D. J. Hepburn (Pacific Search Books, Seattle, 1976).

The Butterflies of the Pacific Northwest, by James R. Christensen (University Press of Idaho, Moscow, Idaho, 1981).

VIRGINIA
The Butterflies Virginia, by Austin H. Clark and Leila F. Clark (Smithsonian Institution, Washington, D.C., 1951).

WASHINGTON
Watching Washington Butterflies, by Robert Michael Pyle (Seattle Audubon Society, 1974).

WESTERN UNITED STATES
A Field Guide to the Western Butterflies, by J. W. Tilden and Arthur C. Smith (Houghton Mifflin Company, Boston, Mass., 1986).

WYOMING
An Annotated Checklist of the Rhopalocera [Butterflies] of Wyoming, by Clifford D. Ferris (Agricultural Experiment Station, University of Wyoming, Laramie, 1971).

CHAPTER FIVE
Butterfly Conservation

Most of us start butterfly gardening as an avocational interest rewarded by being surrounded with beautiful butterflies in our gardens, adding an enjoyable feature to our outside recreational time. But as we become more sensitive to butterflies and their requirements such as nectar sources and larval food plants, we begin to realize that the world is rapidly changing, and not for the better in the case of most butterfly species. The ever-increasing urbanization of our landscape, the sprawl of growing cities and towns, the changing nature of our forests as they are logged, and application of pesticides to control weeds and pest insects, all result in a decreased diversity of butterflies and other wildlife in

The Atala was nearly extinct before a concerted effort by entomologists, horticulturists, and butterfly gardeners revived the species in southern Florida, making it one of the area's most common butterflies.

our world. The butterfly gardener can make a real contribution to increasing both the number of butterflies and the richness of kinds of butterflies in their own area. Let's look at some examples of how butterfly conservation can work hand-in-hand with butterfly gardening.

The Atala Butterfly Story in South Florida

The Atala butterfly (*Eumaeus atala*) is a large and colorful lycaenid butterfly that once inhabited most of the south Florida peninsula and even the northern Keys. They lived primarily in southern pine forests where their larval food plant, the Florida cycad, grew in abundance. As the urbanization of south Florida greatly increased following World War II, many of the pine hammocks (dry areas several feet higher than surrounding marshland or swamps) were cleared for housing. The popularity of the Florida cycad ("coontie") as a starch source also made it a popular plant to collect for culinary purposes. By 1960, the Atala butterfly was extinct on the Florida mainland and restricted to one tiny colony in a state park on Key Biscayne, a small offshore island at the southern edge of Miami Beach. Entomologists tried to establish new colonies by transferring adults and immature stages to the remaining pine hammocks preserved inside Everglades National Park in the mid-1960s, but these efforts came to naught.

The Atala butterfly had nearly become extinct prior to the passage of the Endangered Species Act in 1973, and would have certainly become extinct on August 24, 1992, when the source colony area on Key Biscayne was totally devastated by Hurricane Andrew and wind damage combined with storm surge damage eliminated the former breeding

Butterfly gardeners can help species such as the Schaus' Swallowtail thrive by planting nectar sources and larval host plants, in this case torchwood and wild lime, in their gardens.

grounds there. But fortunately by then the butterfly was widely distributed and thriving on the mainland. Unnoticed by professional lepidopterists and other naturalists, cycads from all over the world had been imported into Dade and Broward counties, from Miami north to Ft. Lauderdale, along with propaga-

tion of the native Florida cycad in many native plant nurseries. Thus in 1979 and 1980, when several south Florida naturalists renewed their efforts to bring the butterfly back to the Florida mainland, the species found a vast resource of potential food plants in the urban areas along the east

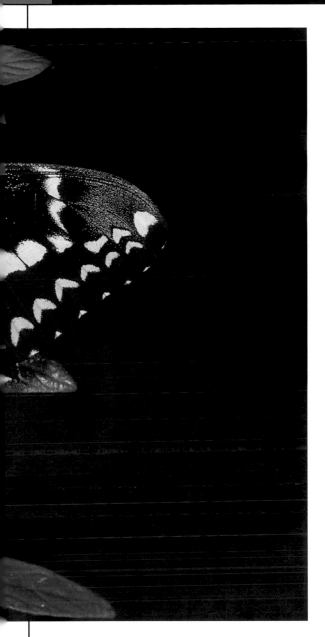

colony of Atala thriving in the owner's back or front yard. This is one of the most remarkable comebacks of a nearly extinct butterfly on record.

Today, the Atala butterfly is one of the "signature" butterflies of southeastern Florida, a species that can be enjoyed by everyone because of its slow flight, conspicuous iridescent blue and green coloration on a black background, and the bright red-orange spots on the underside and on the abdomen of the butterfly.

The Schaus' Swallowtail Story

The Schaus' Swallowtail (*Papilio aristodemus ponceanus*), a large and colorful swallowtail butterfly once native to Florida from the Miami area south to Key West, became extinct on the mainland in 1924 due to clearing of its tropical hardwood hammock habitat because of the expansion of the city of Miami. In the lower and middle Keys, it became extinct by the 1960s due to habitat clearing and pesticide spraying for mosquitoes. In 1972, its last major reserve population on Key Largo suffered a calamity due to the change in spraying protocols by the Monroe County Mosquito Control District to use of second-generation organophosphate sprays (for adult mosquitoes), which reduced the Swallowtail numbers to virtual extinction. The butterfly only survived the next few years on three tiny keys inside Biscayne National Park. By 1984, there were fewer than seventy adult individuals flying for the total species population that flight season. Thus it was placed on the Federal Endangered Species List, and all collecting or other disturbance of the species was strictly prohibited.

By 1990, the effect of mosquito control pesticides on the butterfly had been well-documented by researchers at the University of Florida, and changes in spraying done by the Mosquito Control District in the Keys allowed the butterfly to begin a strong recovery on Key Largo, the largest of the Florida Keys in both land area and tropical hardwood hammock habitat area. But nature had its own potential disaster waiting in the wings in the form of Hurricane Andrew, an extremely strong storm that struck the last remaining habitat areas of the Schaus' Swallowtail on northern Key Largo and the small keys inside Biscayne National Park on August 24, 1992. Fortuitously, two months earlier, our research group at the University of Florida in Gainesville had removed a hundred eggs from wild females to raise in captivity at Gainesville. This small nucleus of a captive colony was carefully nurtured, and by 1995, it was possible to release 760 pupae of the Schaus' Swallowtail at seven new release sites on the mainland and along the length of Key Largo. These were supplemented by another 500 adults being released in 1996 at the same sites.

This butterfly can be helped in its comeback by residents of the Keys planting its two native host plants, torchwood and wild lime, as part of the landscaping of their homes. Likewise, these host plants (which were preserved on the Charles Deering Estate in south Miami) have made possible the reintroduction of the butterfly to the Florida mainland, allowing them to fly on continental United States soil for the first time in more than seventy years. Clearly, a butterfly species can often recover very rapidly if its food plants are available and if other environmental danger-points such as pesticide spraying are alleviated for a while.

coast of south Florida. The Atala butterfly literally exploded in population numbers, becoming one of the commonest butterflies in south Florida by the mid-1980s. Every nursery, botanical garden, and public park with any number of cycads had strong "infestations" of Atala larvae for twelve months a year. Any home that had cycads planted as ornamentals usually had a small

Zinnia elegans ('Ice Cream Yellow') are particularly attractive to many nymphalid butterflies, and Swallowtails and Pierids will also eagerly come to them.

The El Segundo Blue in Southern California

The El Segundo Blue (*Euphilotes battoides allyni*) once inhabited the sand dunes along the southern California coast in Los Angeles County. The popularity of the land these sand dunes occupied for housing, oil company drilling, and expansion of Los Angeles International Airport reduced the butterfly's available habitat to fewer than one hundred acres by the 1960s. Dr. Rudolph H. T. Mattoni of Los Angeles took a personal interest in trying to save this Blue and its endangered habitat, and he mobilized a vast army of volunteers during the 1980s and early 1990s to reclaim parts of the dune habitat for the butterfly. Due to the westward flight path of aircraft taking off from Los Angeles International Airport, many of the former housing areas in the dunes were purchased by the City of Los Angeles, the people moved out, and the houses themselves were removed. Additionally, Chevron Oil Company was willing to cooperate with the biologists who were trying to save this butterfly. On both the airport property and the Chevron reserve, the teams of biologists mobilized by Dr. Mattoni cleared out exotic plants, such as ice plant, which had threatened to take over the dunes, and replanted many of the native nectar sources and larval host plants for the El Segundo Blue.

Today, a thriving population of more than 10,000 El Segundo Blues annually flies in these dunes, a testimony to what applied butterfly gardening and the dedication of committed individuals can accomplish, even in one of the largest cities in the world.

Other Conservation Stories

There are many species of endangered or threatened butterflies in the United States and southern Canada that need attention. The Mitchell Satyr (*Neonympha mitchellii*) in the northeastern United States and Great Lakes Region is now restricted to a few colonies inhabiting wet bogs that have not yet been converted for development use or highway construction. The Bay Area Checkerspot (*Euphydryas editha bayensis*) in the San Francisco Bay area is reduced to a single sizable colony today. It once inhabited hundreds of square miles of the hills surrounding San Francisco Bay, where its larval food plant, *Plantago erecta*, grew in abundance. Today, most of these hills have been converted into housing developments where the plantago no longer grows and the butterfly no longer flies. But other colonies of this species have become extirpated even on privately held, well-protected reserves such as Stanford University's Jasper Ridge Reserve, suggesting that climatic change through global warming (caused ultimately by man's emission of carbon dioxide and other gases into the atmosphere) or air pollution of other types may be having injurious effects on butterfly survival. One can never tell what the role of the private land owner could contribute in this unfolding drama, but it certainly would not hurt to preserve hilltops with *Plantago erecta* and nectar sources on them that the Bay Area Checkerspot could possibly survive in.

There are a dozen species of butterflies on the Federal Endangered Species List in California alone. Most of these Blues, Metalmarks, and Nymphalids are associated with endangered habitats, such as beach dune areas, best left undeveloped for both public recreational use and the conservation of these unique species and the wildflowers and other wildlife that they have been associated with for millennia. In Florida, one third of the butterfly fauna of 160 resident species is estimated to be reduced in distribution to six or fewer populations, again primarily because of land development for orange groves, housing, and other human purposes taking over the wild areas that once existed across the state.

As mentioned in the beginning of this book, Ron Boender of Butterfly World in Coconut Creek, Florida, initiated a campaign several years ago called Bringing Back the Butterflies. He envisions the possibility that if thousands of people took up butterfly gardening and planted not only nectar sources but also the larval food plants across the nation, we could bring many species of butterflies back to urban settings before the local populations become completely extirpated or the species themselves even go to extinction. You can play a very important role in this campaign by not only building your own butterfly garden, but encouraging your neighbors, local schools, county parks department, and commercial businesses to landscape with butterfly nectar sources and butterfly food plants. It is an easy yet dramatically successful way to increase the number of butterflies across North America.

So, while butterfly conservation may not have been the starting point for your venture into butterfly gardening, you can see by this brief series of examples how individuals can make a difference, and how by planting the food plants of butterflies, both for their larvae and for adult stages, you can bring back a species even on the verge of extinction. Good luck in this new and exciting adventure of butterfly gardening!

CHAPTER SIX

Identifying North American Butterflies: A Gallery of Butterflies in Photographs

From the Mexican border to the west coast of the United States and Canada are more than 700 species of butterflies and skippers and approximately 10,000 species of moths. This vast diversity becomes a little overwhelming even for the experts to identify. But fortunately, there are a number of common species that are more likely to be found in most urban and suburban butterfly gardens.

In order to help you identify them, we have included a gallery of photographs of the species you are most likely to see, together with a brief description of their common and scientific names, their ranges across North America, their preferred habitats, and their nectar sources and larval food plants.

The Anise Swallowtail (*Papilio zelicaon*) is a beautiful member of the Swallowtail family that ranges from northern Baja California to British Columbia, and east to the crest of the Rocky Mountains.

BLUES,COPPERS, AND HAIRSTREAKS— LYCAENIDAE

ACMON BLUE
Plebejus acmon

Range: Common throughout the western United States and east across the Great Plains.

Habitat: Open fields, deserts, and drier meadows in woodland areas wherever its food plants are found.

Nectar Sources: Buckwheats, lotus, astragalus, lupines, sweet clover, clover (*Trifolium* species), annual composites in deserts and mountains alike, verbena.

Larval Host Plants: Buckwheat species, lotus, astragalus, lupines, sweet clover.

EASTERN TAILED BLUE
Everes comyntas

Range: Eastern United States and southern Canada, with scattered populations in the West.

Habitat: Disturbed areas, such as fields and roadsides, or mountain meadows along streams, desert foothills, or forest clearings.

Nectar Sources: Bidens and other composites, dogbane, milkweeds.

Larval Host Plants: Legumes, such as astragalus, desmodium, baptisia, lotus, lupines, beans, alfalfa, clovers, and vicia.

The Acmon Blue has a band of silvery blue and orange spots on the hindwing which makes it quite distinctive.

The Eastern Tailed Blue, which looks like a Hairstreak with the two tails protruding off its hind wings, flies east of the Rocky Mountains throughout the spring and summer months.

GRAY HAIRSTREAK
Strymon melinus

Range: Entire United States and southern Canada.

Habitat: Cosmopolitan in open areas, from sea level to the higher mountains.

Nectar Sources: Lemon and other citrus trees, buddleia, composites such as daisies, fleabanes, zinnias, milkweeds.

Larval Host Plants: Herbaceous and occasionally shrubby or arbored species of legumes, including lupines, astragalus, cassia, desmodium, alfalfa, white sweet clover, beans, sweet peas, clovers, vicia; also, mallows such as hibiscus and cultivated cotton; buckwheats, dock (*Rumex* species); rhododendron; lantana; salvia; citrus (lemon); wild rose; and other plants.

GREAT BLUE HAIRSTREAK
Atlides halesus

Range: Southern half of the United States, from California to Florida.

Habitat: Wooded canyons in the West, often around sycamore trees where its mistletoe host plants grow, and in woodland areas in the East, again where its host plants are found.

Nectar Sources: Milkweeds, buddleia, asters and other composites, zinnias, dogbane.

Larval Host Plants: Larvae feed on parasitic mistletoes which in turn grow on poplars, oaks, sycamores, desert shrubs, and conifers such as pines and junipers.

Left: The Gray Hairstreak has a light gray underside with a false "head" at the rear margin of the hindwing, complete with false eye and tails that look like antennae, designed to fool predators.
Right: The Great Blue Hairstreak is one of the largest and most tropical-looking hairstreaks in the North American fauna. The uppersides are a brilliant iridescent blue.

The Juniper Hairstreak can be found breeding on many species of junipers. Adults frequently come to composite flowers near the base of the host trees.

JUNIPER HAIRSTREAK
Mitoura siva

Range: Western half of the United States, from western Texas up through the Rocky Mountain states to Montana and west through Utah and Nevada to central and southern California, Arizona, and New Mexico.

Habitat: Dry or rocky open areas on low mountain slopes wherever junipers occur.

Nectar Sources: Small composites growing in the immediate vicinity of juniper trees.

Larval Host Plants: Western junipers in the genus *Juniperus*.

OLIVE HAIRSTREAK
Mitoura gryneus

Range: Eastern United States, from the eastern Great Plains states to Pennsylvania and New York, south to the extreme northern Florida boundary.

Habitat: Woodland near its favored cedar host trees.

Nectar Sources: Composites, particularly bidens and other daisies, asters. Adults perch on the tops and side branches of the host trees except for brief flights to nearby flowers, so it is especially important to plant both the larval hosts and nectar sources within a few feet of each other.

Larval Host Plants: Eastern cedars in the genus *Juniperus*.

The Silvery Blue is a beautiful spring-flying species named for its very bright blue color on the upperside.

The green underside and a brown upperside of the Olive Hairstreak help it blend to the background when landed on its larval foodplant, eastern cedars.

SILVERY BLUE
Glaucopsyche lygdamus

Range: The Silvery Blue occurs in a variety of races across the western United States to the northeastern part of the United States, and throughout southern Canada north to Alaska.

Habitat: Normally a spring- or early-summer-flying species found in open meadows, gardens, fields, and adjacent woodlands.

Nectar Sources: Mustards, verbena, other small-flowered spring or early summer plants.

Larval Host Plants: The larvae eat the flowers, fruits, and young leaves of a variety of legume species, including astragalus, lotus, lupines, alfalfa, white sweet clover, and vicia. The larvae are tended by ants which drink a sweet honeydew produced by glands on the back of the caterpillars; the ants protect the larvae from enemies such as wasps.

SONORA BLUE
Philotes sonorensis

Range: Southern to central California.

Habitat: Rocky canyons in foothill and lower mountain areas west of the Sierra Nevada Range and throughout the mountain ranges of southern California.

Nectar Sources: Rarely seen nectaring, but will feed on buckwheat flowers and small composites. Adults also visit mud.

Larval Host Plants: Succulent plants in the genus *Dudleya*.

The Sonora Blue is one of the most beautiful blues in the world. The central orange spots on all four wings of the male are extremely distinctive.

The Spring Azure is one of the sure signs of spring, appearing when the first shrubs and legumes bloom.

SPRING AZURE
Celastrina ladon

Range: Eastern United States and southern Canada. Similar species (*Celastrina argiolus*) in the western states up through British Columbia.

Habitat: Wooded areas and meadow edges near them.

Nectar Sources: Many spring-flowering shrubs.

Larval Host Plants: Flowers of spring-flowering shrubs in the rose family; legumes such as lupines, lotus, or sweet clover.

The Western Tailed Blue looks very similar to the Eastern Tailed Blue on the upperside, but can be distinguished by its larger size and chalky white (as opposed to gray) color on the underside.

WESTERN TAILED BLUE
Everes amyntula

Range: Western United States from the Pacific Coast to the Rocky Mountains, and north through western Canada to Alaska.

Habitat: Meadows in chaparral or woodland, open fields, and mountain glades up to the timberline.

Nectar Sources: Asters, daisies, verbena, buddleia, sweet clover.

Larval Host Plants: Herbaceous legumes such as astragalus, oxytropis, and vicia.

63

THE NYMPHS —
NYMPHALIDAE

AMERICAN PAINTED LADY
Vanessa virginiensis

Range: Across the United States and southern Canada, ranging south into the American tropics and the Greater Antilles.

Habitat: Open sunny fields and meadows, from sea level to the higher mountains.

Nectar Sources: Thistles and other composites, buddleia, zinnias, impatiens, lantana, porterweed.

Larval Host Plants: Cudweed, a woolly whitish-leaved plant in the genus *Gnaphalium,* is the favored host, but the butterfly will also use sunflowers, lupines, mallows, nettles, and thistles.

BUCKEYE
Junonia coenia

Range: Entire United States except for the northernmost Rocky Mountain area.

Habitat: Open sunny areas, particularly dry fields with some bare ground on which males can perch and hold territories.

Nectar Sources: Lantana, buddleia, daisies, zinnias, asters, verbena, bidens, and many other composites.

Larval Host Plants: Plantains in the genus *Plantago,* monkeyflowers, snapdragons, gerardia, Indian paintbrush, lippia, verbena.

Above: The American Painted Lady can be quite abundant wherever cudweed, its larval foodplant, grows. Adults prefer purple thistles and buddleia.
Right: The Buckeye has gorgeously colored *ocelli*, or fake eyes, on each wing. Practically every individual is different in exact coloration and pattern, and because of their territoriality and tendency to stay "at home," this species is truly a joy to have established in the garden.

CALIFORNIA TORTOISESHELL
Nymphalis californica

Range: Pacific Coast states, primarily in the mountains, but flies east to the Rocky Mountain states and along the Canadian border to the Great Lakes region.

Habitat: Dry chaparral habitats, oak woodland, ponderosa pine forest, and occasionally higher mountain zones.

Nectar Sources: Thistles and other composites such as asters and daisies. In occasional large migrations in central California, Oregon, and Washington, it may feed on virtually any nectar source.

Larval Host Plants: A number of species of ceanothus shrubs.

The California Tortoiseshell has an orange-brown upperside bordered by black, a pattern which apparently recalled the color and pattern of a tortoiseshell to the person who first coined this common name. The butterfly migrates in huge numbers across western mountain ranges.

The Comma Anglewing has a comma-shaped silver marking on the underside of the hindwing and is commonly found in urban gardens.

COMMA ANGLEWING
Polygonia comma

Range: Eastern half of the United States and Canada, south to the Gulf Coast and northern Florida.

Habitat: Rather cosmopolitan, including urban gardens and woodlands.

Nectar Sources: Thistles and other composites, buddleia; the adults prefer sap and fruit, and will visit rotting apples or peaches on the ground under fruit trees in your garden.

Larval Host Plants: American elm, nettles.

The Diana Fritillary is a highly valued visitor to the butterfly garden in areas of the Southeast and Arkansas that are close to the mountains. The males are bright orange on the outer part of the wing, while the females are bright blue and somewhat larger than the males.

DIANA FRITILLARY
Speyeria diana

Range: Virginia south to northern Georgia and west to Arkansas, in the lower mountain areas.

Habitat: Prefers moist deciduous and pine forests near streams. This spectacular species (orange males and blue females, each marked with black) can normally be found in moist mountain meadows but may be attracted into your butterfly garden if you live within its local range and plant appropriate nectar sources.

Nectar Sources: Thistles, occasionally other mountain composites.

Larval Host Plants: Violets in the genus *Viola* (adults are specific in laying eggs on wild violets, but the larvae can be grown on ordinary garden pansies or the miniature viola species from nursery stock).

GREAT SPANGLED FRITILLARY
Speyeria cybele

There are more than a dozen species of similar-appearing fritillaries in the genus *Speyeria* across the United States. All share violets as larval food plants, and all share thistles and other composites as favored nectaring plants. You can distinguish these similar-appearing species by refering to one or more of the identification manuals suggested in chapter 4.

Range: The northern two thirds of the United States and southern Canada, from near sea level to the higher mountains, in a series of geographically separated races.

Habitat: Open areas adjacent to temperate woodlands in the lowlands or next to mountain conifer forests at higher elevations.

Nectar Sources: Thistles and other composites, mints, milkweed, liatris, purple coneflower, buddleia in the garden.

Larval Host Plants: Violets in the genus *Viola*.

The Great Spangled Fritillary is a representative of the large and complex genus *Speyeria* whose various species occur from Mexico north into Canada. All can be attracted to thistles and all breed on violets.

GULF FRITILLARY
Agraulis vanillae

Range: Breeds in the southern United States, from southern California to the southeastern Gulf states, and migrates north in the summer as far as southern Canada.

Habitat: Open areas, wherever its passionflower larval food plants grow, and also forest margins and suburban gardens and parks.

Nectar Sources: Buddleia, pentas, thistles, bidens and other wild composites, red salvia, verbena, red impatiens, zinnias, daisies, asters, morning glory (Ipomea). Adults occasionally feed at mud.

Larval Host Plants: Passionflowers of the genus *Passiflora*.

The Gulf Fritillary will literally take over your garden if you plant a number of passionflowers along a fence or trellis. It will even breed as far north as Delaware in the summer, given a supply of its host plant in your garden there.

The Meadow Fritillary is one of the most widely distributed of the smaller fritillary species. Adults come to a number of species of composites.

MEADOW FRITILLARY
Boloria bellona

There are many species of Meadow Fritillaries in the Rocky Mountain states, the Pacific Northwest, the Great Lakes states, and Canada. Most of these are restricted to higher elevations where they fly in willow bogs or moist habitats. People with mountain homes may attract these butterflies to their garden in numbers if they plant an abundance of asters, thistles or other composites as nectar sources.

Range: The northern United States and southern Canada. Occurs as far south as Missouri, Kentucky, North Carolina, and Virginia in the eastern United States, and Colorado in the western United States.

Habitat: Moist or wet meadows in pine forest or higher mountain areas.

Nectar Sources: Asters and other composites.

Larval Host Plants: Several species of violets.

MILBERT'S TORTOISESHELL
Nymphalis milberti

Range: From the Pacific Coast of the United States, Canada, and Alaska, east to the Atlantic Coast across the northern tier of states, with extensions southward in the Great Basin ranges and Rocky Mountains.

Habitat: Forest glades and open meadows, usually in moist situations where the larval host plant grows.

Nectar Sources: Shrubby cinquefoil, thistles and other composites such as fleabane, other asters, and daisies, ocassionally fermenting sap as on injured yucca flowers.

Larval Host Plants: Stinging nettles (easily grown in a moist area of your butterfly garden).

MONARCH
Danaus plexippus

Range: All of North America except northern Canada and Alaska. For the western monarch population, the winter range contracts to several dozen overwintering sites along the California coast or Saline Valley in California's Great Basin desert. For the eastern United States and Canadian populations, the major overwintering sites are located in central Mexico. The wider North American range is reoccupied each spring by migrants coming north from these overwintering colonies of adults.

Habitat: Cosmopolitan, although prefers open areas such as fields, gardens, and meadows.

Nectar Sources: Milkweeds, buddleia, lantana, thistles and other composites, zinnias, asters, daisies, dogbane.

Larval Host Plants: At least 26 of the 108 species of milkweeds found north of the Mexican border serve as larval host plants.

The black spiny larvae of Milbert's Tortoishell, which is quite distinctive in its adult stage with its orange and yellow wing bands, are found on stinging nettles.

Left: The adult Monarch female has a uniformly black-veined hindwing, whereas the male has an enlarged black spot containing scent scales in the center of the hindwing.

Top right: About 24 hours before a Monarch adult is ready to emerge from the pupa, the pupal case becomes transparent and one can see the adult wing pattern through it.

Bottom right: After it breaks free of the transparent shell, the adult pumps fluid into its wings and, as the abdomen slowly decreases in size, the wings elongate to their full extent.

MOURNING CLOAK
Nymphalis antiopa

Range: Entire United States, Canada, and Alaska, as well as eastern Mexico south to Venezuela, and across Europe into Asia.

Habitat: Normally deciduous woodland or suburban gardens, preferring cooler climates of the mountains in the tropics or subtropics north in both mountains and lowlands to the edge of the arctic tundra.

Nectar Sources: The Mourning Cloak feeds at oozing sap from injuries to the trunks of trees or branches, damaged or fermenting fruit, and nectar from thistles, hollyhocks, or other large, deep-corolla flowers.

Larval Host Plants: Willows, elms, quaking aspen and other poplars, ash, wild rose, beech, hackberry, maples.

PAINTED LADY
Vanessa cardui

Range: Cosmopolitan across North America, northern Africa, Europe, and Pacific Islands.

Habitat: Open sunny habitats from deserts below sea level to the highest mountains. In North America, the species is a notable migrant, breeding through the winter in northern Mexico and moving north each spring in a succession of broods. The butterfly does not survive the winter north of the frost line, and a partial southward migration occurs in the fall.

Nectar Sources: Thistles and other composites, buddleia, zinnias, pentas, and a wide variety of native wildflowers from the deserts to the alpine zones.

Larval Host Plants: Thistles of many species and an extraordinarily wide variety of weedy herbaceous plants (sunflowers, yarrow, mallows, wild cotton, lupines, beans, clovers, petunia, mustards, etc.) found in open or disturbed areas.

The Mourning Cloak, here shown hanging from its pupal shell, is one of the first butterflies to appear in the spring. Adults can overwinter in hollow logs and become active on the first warm days.

The Painted Lady is a renowned migrant that may be found in almost any part of North America during the late spring and summer months.

The Question Mark has a silver mark shaped like a question sign on its underside, from whence it gets its common and scientific names.

QUESTION MARK
Polygonia interrogationis

Range: Eastern United States and southern Canada, from the Rocky Mountains to the Atlantic Coast, including the Florida peninsula.

Habitat: Deciduous woodlands with open meadows and glades, as well as suburban gardens.

Nectar Sources: Feeds on thistles and other composites, but like most Anglewings in the genus *Polygonia,* it feeds on oozing sap and fruits normally, when not seeking nectar sources.

Larval Host Plants: American elm and other Ulmus species, hackberry trees, nettle.

RED ADMIRAL
Vanessa atalanta

Range: All of North America, Europe, and northern Asia.

Habitat: Open, sunny fields, gardens, and mountain meadows, from deserts to the edge of the arctic tundra.

Nectar Sources: Thistles and other compostites, zinninas, buddleia, butterfly weed and other milkweeds, lilac, pentas, marigolds.

Larval Host Plants: Nettles are favored food plants of the larvae.

The Red Admiral is found across the northern hemisphere in North America and Europe, where both adults and larvae feed on thistles.

RED-SPOTTED PURPLE
Limenitis astyanax

Range: Eastern United States, from northern Florida to southern Canada.

Habitat: Deciduous woodland areas and fields adjacent to streams or forests.

Nectar Sources: Thistles, buddleia, zinnias, milkweeds. The adults also avidly visit sap from trees, fruits, animal droppings, carrion, or even decaying wood.

Larval Host Plants: Willow trees, poplars.

The Red-spotted Purple has shiny blue markings on the hindwing, discouraging enemies because of its resemblance to the Pipevine Swallowtail. Sometimes this butterfly and the White-banded Admiral hybridize and form intermediately colored butterflies as offspring.

The Variegated Fritillary is found across much of the United States during the summer, even high into the Colorado Rockies.

VARIEGATED FRITILLARY
Euptoieta claudia

Range: United States, east of the Sierra Nevada and Cascade ranges, and southern Canada, even in the higher mountains such as the Rockies or Appalachians, during the summer. Breeds across the southern states.

Habitat: Found in open areas, including grassland, agricultural fields, deserts, and mountain meadows up to 10,000 feet (3,050m) elevation.

Nectar Sources: Zinnias, thistles, bidens, and other composites.

Larval Host Plants: Violets, linum, passionflower, plantago.

WEIDEMEYER'S ADMIRAL
Limenitis weidemeyerii

Range: Rocky Mountain states west across the Great Basin to eastern California, southeastern Oregon, and southwestern Canada.

Habitat: Willow-lined streams, from the edge of the desert to the higher mountains, and frequently along wooded mountain canyons, aspen groves, and moist mountain meadows in the Rockies and the eastern Sierra Nevada Range.

Nectar Sources: Thistles and other composites such as asters, shrubby cinquefoil, buddleia, zinnias. Adults also feed on tree sap, drink at mud, and visit carrion or dung.

Larval Host Plants: Willow trees, quaking aspen.

VICEROY
Limenitis archippus

Range: Entire United States except west of the Sierra Nevada and Cascade ranges, with desert races in Arizona and extreme southeastern California.

Habitat: Willow-lined streams (even in deserts) and ponds, or nearby moist meadow areas and deciduous woodland.

Nectar Sources: Buddleia, thistles, zinnias, bidens, and other composites, dogbane, lilac, pentas, occasionally red impatiens.

Larval Host Plants: Willow trees, poplars.

Above: The Viceroy occurs across much of the United States, mimicking the Monarch and Queen in general color pattern. All three butterflies are distasteful to birds. Right: Weidemeyer's Admiral prefers aspens, its larval foodplant, but will eat nectar from thistles and other composites or even lilacs.

WHITE-BANDED ADMIRAL
Limenitis arthemis

Range: Northeastern United States and eastern Canada.

Habitat: Deciduous woodland areas and moist meadows adjacent to forests.

Nectar Sources: Thistles, buddleia, zinnias, milkweeds. Like the Red-Spotted Purple, the adults also avidly visit sap from trees, fruits, animal droppings, carrion, or even decaying wood.

Larval Host Plants: Willows, poplars, beech.

WEST COAST LADY
Vanessa carye

Range: Pacific Coast states, east to the Rocky Mountains and north into southwestern Canada.

Habitat: Open areas, fields, and suburbs from the southern California coast to fir forests high in the mountains.

Nectar Sources: Verbena, thistles, sunflowers, and other composites.

Larval Host Plants: Mallows are the favored hosts in most urban and suburban situations.

Left: The White-banded Admiral prefers wooded areas around willows and poplars where it can readily lay its eggs.
Above: The West Coast Lady can be distinguished from the Painted Lady by its small blue hindwing spots and shorter, broader forewings.

ZEPHYR ANGLEWING
Polygonia zephyrus

Range: Western half of the United States, from the Rocky Mountains to the Pacific and western Canada.

Habitat: Primarily meadows and open woods in mountain situations, from ponderosa pine forests to Canadian-zone fir forests. Likes to land on sunlit fallen logs in forest glades and open meadows.

Nectar Sources: Shrubby cinquefoil, thistles and other composites, gooseberry bushes.

Larval Host Plants: Gooseberry, currants.

A pair of mating Zebra Heliconians hang from a lantana flower.

ZEBRA HELICONIAN
Heliconius charitonius

Range: Southern United States, from the Southeast to southern Arizona; occasionally migrates north in the summertime to Nebraska and Missouri.

Habitat: Usually found along the open edges of woodlands where the larval host plants grow.

Nectar Sources: Bidens and other composites, buddleia, salvia, pentas, and red-orange impatiens.

Larval Host Plants: Passionflowers in the genus *Passiflora*.

The Zephyr Anglewing has a distinctly gray, bark-textured underside and a tawny orange upperside that camouflage the butterfly quite nicely in the woods.

THE SKIPPERS— HESPERIIDAE

COMMON CHECKERED SKIPPER
Pyrgus communis

Range: Eastern United States and southern Canada.

Habitat: Open weedy areas such as fields and urban vacant lots.

Nectar Sources: Mallows, lantana, buddleia, asters, zinnias, daisies, bidens.

Larval Host Plants: Mallows, hibiscus, and their relatives.

FIERY SKIPPER
Hylephila phyleus

Range: Across the United States including the Northeast, and Florida to southern California, excepting only the northwestern quadrant of the United States.

Habitat: Open, grassy areas such as lawns, where adults frequently perch, and also weedy margins of woodland and roadsides.

Nectar Sources: Lantana, buddleia, daisies, thistles, asters, dogbane, milkweeds, bidens, and other weedy composites; lemon trees and other citrus flowers.

Larval Host Plants: Grasses, including Bermuda grass, Kentucky blue grass, and other common lawn grasses.

Above: The Common Checkered Skipper is found everywhere east of the Rocky Mountains. It particularly likes mallows for both nectar and larval feeding.
Right: The male of the Fiery Skipper is bright orange marked with black, while the female is a duller brown color.

Long-tailed Skipper larvae can sometimes be pests in commercial bean fields, but are delightful visitors to private gardens.

LONG-TAILED SKIPPER
Urbanus proteus

Range: Southeastern United States from Florida to Texas (north to the mid-Atlantic states), and in the Southwest, along the Mexican border to southern California.

Habitat: Urban gardens, open fields, roadsides, and edges of wooded areas.

Nectar Sources: Bidens and other composites, zinnias, asters, daisies, buddleia, pentas, milkweeds.

Larval Host Plants: Herbaceous legumes, such as clitoria, desmodium, beans, mesquite, wisteria.

SACHEM
Atalopedes campestris

Range: Breeds throughout the southern half of the United States, from the Atlantic Coast to California and north there to Oregon. In the central states, adults migrate as far north as North Dakota and Ontario by late summer.

Habitat: Open grassy areas and weedy roadsides or woodland edges.

Nectar Sources: Bidens and other weedy composites, buddleia, lemon and other citrus flowers, zinnias, daisies, asters, dogbane.

Larval Host Plants: Grasses, including Bermuda grass and Festuca species of lawn grasses.

The male Sachem has a very large black patch of scent scales in the middle of the forewing, while on the underside it is mostly yellow, with a vague band of paler hindwing spots.

The Silver-spotted Skipper is named for the large silver spot on the underside of its hindwing. It is one of the largest skipper species, commonly reaching over two inches (5cm) in wingspread.

SILVER-SPOTTED SKIPPER
Epargyreus clarus

Range: Almost the entire United States and southern Canada, although more commonly distributed in the eastern United States.

Habitat: Weedy fields, grassy meadows, and open woodland.

Nectar Sources: Buddleia, lantana, pentas, zinnias, asters and other composites. Adults also visit mud to drink.

Larval Host Plants: A variety of legumes, including robinia, acacia, desmodium, lotus, beans, and wisteria.

SNOUTS — LIBYTHEIDAE

SNOUT BUTTERFLY
Libytheana bachmanii

Range: Breeding populations across the southern United States from southeastern California desert to Florida and north to Virginia, sporadic or migrating northward to the Canadian border excluding only the Pacific Northwest.

Habitat: Lowland areas such as desert and subtropical scrub in the Southwest, and open areas in deciduous woodland in the East.

Nectar Sources: Lantana, verbena, buddleia, bidens, and other composites.

Larval Host Plants: Hackberry trees of the genus *Celtis.*

The Snout Butterfly is so-called be-cause of the long "palpi" projecting off the front of its face on either side of the proboscis, or tongue.

SWALLOWTAILS—PAPILIONIDAE

ANISE SWALLOWTAIL
Papilio zelicaon

Range: From the Pacific Coast states and western Canada to the eastern side of the crest of the Rocky Mountains.

Habitat: This butterfly can be found from sea level along the coast or interior deserts to 14,000 feet (4,270 meters) in the California Sierra Nevada range or the Rocky Mountains. It is most commonly seen in the springtime in foothill areas and vacant city lots, where wild anise or fennel plants are growing.

Nectar Sources: The Anise Swallowtail avidly feeds on thistles, asters, lantana, zinnias, and other common garden flowers.

Larval Host Plants: Members of the carrot family, including fennel, anise, carrots, parsley, and various genera of wild umbellifers (members of the carrot family, the Umbelliferae).

EASTERN BLACK SWALLOWTAIL
Papilio polyxenes

Range: Primarily from the Rocky Mountains east to the Atlantic Coast of southern Canada and United States, although penetrating into the Southwest in Arizona and extreme southeastern California.

Habitat: This swallowtail prefers open, weedy fields and roadsides, where its favored larval food plants of the carrot family grow.

Nectar Sources: Adults feed on thistles, asters and other composites, zinnias, impatiens, buddleia, pentas, milkweed, bee balm, phlox, purple coneflower, and liatris.

Larval Host Plants: Members of the carrot family, including dill, fennel, wild anise, carrot, parsley, Queen Anne's lace, wild parsnip, rue, and their relatives.

Left: The underside and upperside of the Anise Swallowtail are very similar in coloration and pattern.
Right: The Eastern Black Swallowtail has larvae that are yellowish-green with transverse black bands and yellow or orange dots on these bands. The adults, like this female, have the general coloring of the distasteful Pipevine Swallowtail.

EASTERN TIGER SWALLOWTAIL
Papilio glaucus

Range: The eastern half of the United States and southern Canada, from the Rocky Mountains to the Atlantic Ocean and the Gulf of Mexico.

Habitat: This yellow Swallowtail, with narrow, short black stripes, prefers moist deciduous forests and open park areas, such as roadways and trails, adjacent to deciduous trees.

Nectar Sources: Buddleia, purple thistles, rhododendron, ixora, lilac, pentas, red impatiens, milkweed, liatris, phlox, purple coneflower, and composites (Joe pye weed, ironweed). Adult males will come to mud puddles.

Larval Host Plants: Wild cherry, tulip tree, beech, sweet bay magnolia, sassafras, ash, prickly ash *(Zanthoxylum americanum)*, quaking aspen.

The Eastern Tiger Swallowtail was named two centuries ago by Linnaeus from material sent to him out of Georgia. It is the most common and most widely distributed eastern Swallowtail butterfly in the United States.

GIANT SWALLOWTAIL
Papilio cresphontes

Range: The eastern half of the United States and southern Canada, from the Rocky Mountains to the Atlantic Ocean, and southward to Texas and Arizona and the Great Central Valley of California.

Habitat: This swallowtail prefers open, sunny areas with lots of flowers.

Nectar Sources: Bougainvilla, zinnias, composites and various daisies, pentas, impatiens, buddleia, liatris, and phlox.

Larval Host Plants: This species is known as "Orange Dog" in the South, because its large caterpillars feed on orange trees and other citrus. It also feeds on wild lime, prickly ash, Hercules club, and related species in the genus *Zanthoxylem.*

The Giant Swallowtail is the largest Swallowtail in the United States. The bird-dropping-colored larvae are pests on citrus in some areas of the country.

The Palamedes Swallowtail is typically found near swampy woods in the southeastern United States, and has either two or three broods of adults a year. It has a striped abdomen, rather than spotted as the Spicebush Swallowtail, and is a part of the complex of Swallowtails believed to resemble the Pipevine Swallowtail for protection against their enemies.

PALAMEDES SWALLOWTAIL
Papilio palamedes

Range: The coastal plain of the southeastern United States, especially the Deep South along the Gulf Coast.

Habitat: Moist deciduous woods, especially swampy areas.

Nectar Sources: Thistles, buddleia, pentas, asters, impatiens, ixora, morning glory (Ipomea), azalea, rhododendron, and composites (ironweed, joe pye weed).

Larval Host Plants: Sassafras, persea trees.

PIPEVINE SWALLOWTAIL
Battus philenor

Range: Most of the United States south of the frostline, including interior valleys and deserts of California, Arizona, southern Colorado, Texas to Florida, and north in the eastern United States to at least Virginia in breeding populations.

Habitat: Usually in wooded areas or brush, occasionally oak-grassland (especially in northern California).

Nectar Sources: Milkweed, pentas, buddleia, zinnias, sweet clover, morning glory (Ipomea), and roadside composites such as bidens.

Larval Host Plants: Pipevines in the genus *Aristolochia*.

The Pipevine Swallowtail is distasteful to birds because of poisonous chemicals incorporated by its caterpillars from pipevines, the larval foodplant. Here the female of a mating pair spreads her wings and shows her iridescent blue-green sheen.

SPICEBUSH SWALLOWTAIL
Papilio troilus

Range: From the Rocky Mountains to the Atlantic Ocean and south to the Gulf of Mexico, thus including most of the eastern United States and southern Canada.

Habitat: This Swallowtail prefers forested areas and the edges of fields and gardens.

Nectar Sources: Buddleia, pentas, zinnias, impatiens, thistles, morning glory (Ipomea).

Larval Host Plants: Spicebush is the preferred host, but sassafras, camphor, tulip tree, and sweet bay magnolia *(Magnolia virginiana)* will also suffice.

WESTERN TIGER SWALLOWTAIL
Papilio rutulus

Range: Pacific Coast of the United States and the southwestern corner of Canada east to the crest of the Rocky Mountains.

Habitat: This yellow Swallowtail, with wide, long black stripes, flies in green city parks and backyard gardens, desert mountain canyons, deciduous woodland, and willow-lined streams in pine forests.

Nectar Sources: California wild lilac, buddleia, pentas, red impatiens, thistles, rhododendron. Adult males will congregate at mud puddles.

Larval Host Plants: Willow, quaking aspen, elm, maple, sycamore.

Left: The Spicebush Swallowtail, widespread across the eastern United States, usually flies in shady woods near its foodplants or visits flowers in open gardens and fields. The male is shown here; the females very closely resemble the Pipevine Swallowtail.
Right: The Western Tiger Swallowtail is generally a little smaller than the Eastern Tiger Swallowtail, and has broader, longer black stripes on the wings together with larger marginal yellow spots.

The Zebra Swallowtail flies in southern gardens during the middle part of the day and afternoon hours. Their long tails dance like floating paddles in the breeze behind the rapidly fluttering, zebra-striped wings.

ZEBRA SWALLOWTAIL
Eurytides marcellus

Range: Eastern United States, from the Gulf of Mexico to southern Canada.

Habitat: Prefers moist deciduous forest near streams, ponds, and swamps, but in the early spring in northern Florida, occurs in dry pine forest in sandhills.

Nectar Sources: Not commonly seen nectaring, but attracted to white-colored buddleia, pentas, and other garden flowers. Adults visit mud to drink. This swallowtail has a short proboscis, so it needs to feed on flowers with a short tube length or flat head, such as cherry (Prunus), malus, or blackberry.

Larval Host Plants: Shrubs in the genus *Asimina*, especially *A. triloba*.

WHITES AND SULPHURS— PIERIDAE

BARRED SULPHUR
Eurema daira

Range: Southern United States, from southeastern Arizona and eastern Texas to Florida and north along the Atlantic Coast.

Habitat: Open weedy areas from deserts to subtropical brushland, and edges of deciduous woodland or southern pine forest.

Nectar Sources: Bidens and other composites, Mexican heather, indigo bush. Adults also visit mud.

Larval Host Plants: Various herbaceous legumes such as aeschynomeme, beggar's tick (desmodium), stylosanthes, and cassia, occasionally mimosa.

Mating pairs of Barred Sulphurs will rest for a half hour here on pentas while the male transfers his package of sperm to the female.

CABBAGE WHITE
Pieris rapae

Range: Across the United States and southern Canada, from the Mexican border northward.

Habitat: Originally introduced into Quebec in about 1860 from Europe, the Cabbage White has spread across the United States and can be found in almost every habitat, even the higher mountains.

Nectar Sources: Feeds avidly at mustards, zinnias, marigolds, thistles and other composites with fairly short flower tubes, buddleia, and lantana.

Larval Host Plants: Practically any member of the mustard family (Cruciferae), such as yellow mustard, cabbage, rape, nasturtium, radishes, etc.

The California Dogface has a splash of iridescent purple across the yellow area of the forewing in the male, while the female is practically pure lemon yellow.

The Cabbage White butterfly is dusted with yellow and gray scaling on the underside of the hindwings. The forewing bears either one large black spot (male) or two black spots (female).

CALIFORNIA DOGFACE
Zerene eurydice

Range: Southern California north in the Central Valley to the foothills of northern California.

Habitat: Normally in the foothills and lower mountains of southern California (in open fields and chaparral) and in oak-grassland and transition-zone pine forest in northern California.

Nectar Sources: California buckeye, wild lilac, thistles, red penstemons, and garden flowers such as red salvia, pentas, and buddleia when planted within its range.

Larval Host Plants: The legume *Amorpha californica.*

Larval Host Plants: Various *Cassia* species of legumes, including both annual herbs and perennial shrubs.

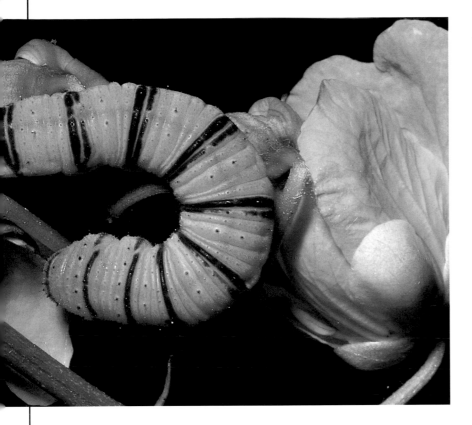

COMMON DOGFACE
Zerene cesonia

Range: Breeds across the southern United States from Florida and the Atlantic Coast to Arizona, and occurs intermittently north through central California to North Dakota and the northeastern United States.

Habitat: Open fields, grassland, and even desert areas at lower altitudes.

Nectar Sources: Buddleia, zinnias, bidens and other composites, pentas, red impatiens.

Larval Host Plants: Legumes such as amorpha, alfalfa, clovers.

CLOUDLESS GIANT SULPHUR
Phoebis sennae

Range: Entire southern half of the United States, from California to Florida and north to Colorado, South Dakota, Wisconsin, and even New York and Maine in favorable summers.

Habitat: Open, sunny areas, including gardens and parks. This species is highly migratory and moves north across the United States from its overwintering sites in western Mexico, southern Texas, and southern Florida during the spring, and south again by the millions in the fall.

Nectar Sources: Pentas, buddleia, lantana, daisies, zinnias, butterfly bush and other milkweeds, lilac, impatiens (especially red and red-orange cultivars), morning glory (Ipomea), and azaleas.

Larval Host Plants: Various *Cassia* species of legumes, including both annual herbs and perennial shrubs.

Left: The larva of the Cloudless Giant Sulphur, with alternating stripes of yellow and black and scattered black dots, avidly devours Cassia leaves and flowers.
Above: In mating butterflies such as this pair of Common Dogfaces, the undersides look very similar. However, the male has a lemon yellow upperside with broad black borders; the female has yellow patches breaking up the bold black border.

COMMON SULPHUR
Colias philodice

Range: Found across most of the United States and Canada, except for Florida and California west of the Sierra Nevada range.

Habitat: Open grassy meadows where its larval host plants grow; also abundant in alfalfa fields.

Nectar Sources: Clover, asters, zinnias, and other short flower-length plants.

Larval Host Plants: Clover species (*Trifolium*), alfalfa, astragalus, lotus, lupines, and other legumes.

COMMON OR CHECKERED WHITE
Pontia protodice

Range: Across most of the United States, from deserts into the higher mountains, except for the Pacific Northwest.

Habitat: Generally found in open weedy areas wherever mustards grow. Easily attracted to the garden if you plant mustards, cabbage, radishes, or similar plants as border ornamentals and let them flower.

Nectar Sources: Mustard flowers, buddleia, daisies and other composites.

Larval Host Plants: Various mustard species.

Above: The wings of the male Common Sulphur have a solid color border, while the female's border is broken up with yellow spots. Right: The Common or Checkered White has a rectangular spot along the middle of each forewing edge. The undersides have a light greenish-yellow, brown zigzag or checkered pattern.

DAINTY YELLOW
Nathalis iole

Range: Southern United States, from Florida to Arizona and southern California, and north in the summertime to the Pacific Northwest, east of the Cascades, and the Canadian border east to the Atlantic Coast. In the summer, the species reaches timberline at 10,500 feet (3,200m) in the Colorado Rockies.

Habitat: Open areas such as fields, deserts, meadows, and roadsides.

Nectar Sources: Bidens and other white and yellow composites, zinnias, asters.

Larval Host Plants: Field and roadside weeds in the composite family, such as bidens, cosmos, and dyssodia.

A Dainty Yellow sips nectar from a composite at the Santa Anna Wildlife Refuge in Texas.

FALCATE ORANGETIP
Anthocharis midea

In contrast to the Sara Orangetip, which is orange-tipped in both sexes, the Falcate Orangetip male butterfly has orange wingtips, while its female mate is entirely white.

Range: From the eastern slope of the Rocky Mountains to the Atlantic Coast and south to northern Florida and Texas.

Habitat: Moist meadows and forests or garden areas surrounded by woodland.

Nectar Sources: Small spring flowers such as mustards.

Larval Host Plants: Mustard species such as *Arabis, Cardamine, Sisymbrium,* and *Dentaria.*

The underside of the Falcate Orangetip of both sexes (female, right; male, below) is delicately mottled with green formed by a mixture of yellow and black scales on the white wing background. The topsides of the wings differ between the sexes.

LARGE ORANGE SULPHUR
Phoebis agarithe

Range: South-central United States, from southern Florida and Louisiana west through Texas and New Mexico to southern Arizona, occasionally north in the Great Plains as far as southern Wisconsin and Michigan.

Habitat: Found primarily in the subtropical areas of the Gulf Coast, this species also ranges into the desert mountain canyons of the Southwest.

Nectar Sources: Pentas, buddleia, composites such as zinnias and bidens.

Larval Host Plants: Various legumes, including pithecellobium and occasionally cassia.

The Large Orange Sulphur is one of the more spectacular sulphur species that one can attract to a butterfly garden. With its bright wings, it is a thrilling sight as it visits the purple pentas or composites.

The Orange Sulphur, or Alfalfa Butterfly, is bright orange on the upperside in the summer and fall, while in spring, it may have substantial yellow on the upperside of the wings with an orange spot remaining in the center.

ORANGE SULPHUR (ALFALFA BUTTERFLY)
Colias eurytheme

Range: Across the United States and southern Canada, from coast to coast and at all altitudes.

Habitat: Open grassy fields and cultivated alfalfa fields.

Nectar Sources: Alfalfa, zinnias, bidens, and other composites.

Larval Host Plants: Alfalfa plants (which can be easily planted in the garden from seed obtainable at your local agricultural supply store); astragalus, lotus, cassia, white sweet clover (*Melilotus alba*), and clovers.

ROSY MARBLE
Euchloe olympia

Range: Eastern half of the United States, starting in central eastern Texas and expanding northward from the Rocky Mountain states to Michigan; Ontario in Canada.

Habitat: Meadows, prairies, and open deciduous woodland or even foothill chaparral (in Colorado).

Nectar Sources: Various mustard species.

Larval Host Plants: Mustard species, including *Arabis, Sisymbrium,* and *Descurainia.*

The underside of the Rosy Marble has broadly scattered marbling distinct from any of the Orangetip species due to the breadth of the bands and the lack of diffuse darker scaling across the hindwing which is found in the Orangetips.

The Sara Orangetip is immediately distinguishable by the bright orange forewing tips on the male and the smaller orange patch surrounded by black and white on the forewings of the female.

SARA ORANGETIP
Anthocharis sara

Range: From the Rocky Mountains west to the Pacific Coast, occurring in a number of geographic subspecies and seasonal forms during the early spring to summer months.

Habitat: Open grassy hillsides or widely scattered woodland, including chaparral in California and western Colorado.

Nectar Sources: Mustards and small composite flowers.

Larval Host Plants: Mustard species, such as *Arabis* and *Sisymbrium;* occasionally nasturtium in gardens.

SLEEPY ORANGE
Eurema nicippe

Range: Southern United States from Florida and the Atlantic Coast states to California.

Habitat: Open fields, deciduous woodland, and second-growth areas.

Nectar Sources: Buddleia, zinnias, bidens and other composites, salvia, penstemon, purple or blue porterweed. Adults also visit mud.

Larval Host Plants: Various species of cassia and related legumes.

This Sleepy Orange female has just emerged from its pupa; its wings are not yet fully expanded and dried for flight.

SOUTHERN WHITE
Ascia monuste

Range: Southeastern United States, from Florida to Texas and southeastern Arizona; breeds only in southern Florida and southern Texas.

Habitat: Often found along the coast, flying in great numbers during migrations which are mainly a result of crowding.

Nonmigratory individuals move relatively little and may be found in the same areas as the migrants.

Nectar Sources: Bidens and other roadside composites, zinnias, buddleia, pentas, milkweeds.

Larval Host Plants: Batis, capers (i.e., *Cleome*), and mustards or crucifers such as *Brassica* and *Lepidium* or *Nasturtium*.

VIRGINIA WHITE
Pieris virginiensis

Range: Throughout much of the northeastern United States and adjacent southeastern Canada, south through the Appalachian Mountains to northern Georgia.

Habitat: Deciduous woods, particularly in the transition zone of the mountains.

Nectar Sources: Mustard flowers, other small delicate wildflowers.

Larval Host Plants: Mustard species, such as *Arabis* and *Sisymbrium*, occassionally nasturtium in gardens.

Left: The Southern White favors the beach areas of the southeastern United States, but may be found inland in the southern parts of Florida, Texas, and Arizona.
Right: The Virginia White is found more in wooded areas than either the Cabbage White or Checkered White species, and flies a little more delicately and slowly than its two more urban sister species.

GLOSSARY OF TERMS

Abdomen   The third principal body segment of the adult and posterior section of the larva.

Antenna (plural – antennae)
One of the two long, knobbed "feelers" extending out from the front or the top of the head of a butterfly. These have receptor organs on them to detect flower scents, perfume scents from the opposite sex, and even food plant scents of the host plant for the eggsand larvae.

Caterpillar   The larval stage of a butterfly, normally completely herbivorous (the larvae of a few Blue species are carnivorous on ant larvae).

Chrysalis (plural – chrysalises)
The pupa or resting stage of a butterfly; the third stage of a butterfly's metamorphosis.

Egg   The first stage of a butterfly's life history; usually, several hundred eggs are laid by a mated female, but some Sulphurs, such as the Orange Sulphur, are capable of producing up to 1,400 eggs during their lifetime.

Head   The first of three major body segments of the butterfly or larva, containing a small brain, two large compound eyes of several thousand facets, and a long coiled tongue or proboscis at the front, through which the butterfly sucks nectar.

Larva (plural – larvae)   The caterpillar, or second stage of the butterfly's metamorphosis, usually herbivorous (one lycaenid caterpillar in the United States is carnivorous and eats aphids; a few other lycaenids eat ant larvae).

Metamorphosis   The life cycle of a butterfly; in this order of insects, each species goes through a complete metamorphosis, from egg to larva to pupa to adult.

Nectar   A sugar-rich secretion from specialized glands in a plant's flowers (and occasionally at the base of leaves in special foliar nectaries), which may also contain free amino acids and other nutrients attractive to butterflies. The plant uses this nectar reward to bring pollinators such as butterflies to its flowers, so that the pollen will be transferred from one flower to another flower by the flying insect and the plants will be cross-pollinated.

Pollen   A protein-rich mass of grains on the anthers of a flower; each pollen grain contains two sperm cells internally. The outside of the pollen grain contains proteins and other food items that attract certain butterflies such as Heliconius (the Zebra). These few butterfly species that have learned to gather pollen will visit several plants, packing pollen on the outside of their proboscis, before they stop somewhere to digest their meal by secreting gut enzymes

out of the proboscis tip onto the mass of pollen, and then sucking in the digested pollen proteins an hour later. During these visits, pollination between plants may be effected.

Proboscis (plural – probosces)
The tongue of the butterfly, composed of two closely pressed halves with a hollow center, through which the butterfly sucks nectar via a vacuum created by a sucking pump in the head.

Pupa   The "resting" stage of the butterfly's metamorphosis or life cycle, in which the final changes from larval tissues to adult issues are completed.

Thorax   The middle section of the butterfly's body in both the adult and larva (composed of three subsections in each case), containing the heart (an enlarged vessel at the top of the body), wing muscles, and bases for the six legs of the adult and the front three pairs of legs for the larva.

Wings   The four membranous, paddlelike extensions from the thorax that carry the adult butterfly's weight in flight; normally, they are covered with pigmented scales (resulting from expanded hairs) which generate the rich coloration of the butterfly's pattern.

Left: A mature Monarch larva munches away on a milkweed (*Asclepias*) flower, deviating slightly from its usual meal of the milkweed leaves.

©Greg R. Ballmer: p. 62 left

©Jaret C. Daniels: pp. 36, 62 right, 95, 97 right

Dembinsky Photo Associates: ©Sharon Cummings: pp. 65; ©John Gerlach: pp. 80 left, 81 right; ©Randall B. Henne: p. 98 left; ©Gary Meszaros: pp. 71, 75; ©Skip Moody: pp. 64, 73 top center, 74, 102; ©Richard Shiell: p. 86

©Thomas C. Emmel: pp. 48, 50-51, 100 top

©Dency Kane: pp. 1 top, 3 bottom, 12, 13, 17, 20 top & bottom, 21 left & right, 22, 24 top & bottom, 26 right, 32 top & right, 33, 34, 38, 46, 52

©George O. Krizek: pp. 2, 48, 57, 61 left, 76 right, 79 right, 82 left, 83 left & right, 103, 106, 107

©Charles Mann: pp. 8, 10, 11, 16, 25, 26 left, 32 left, 37

©James L. Nation, Jr.: p. 72

©Edward Ross: pp. 40, 42, 59, 60, 63, 66, 80 top, 82 right, 85, 91, 93, 96 left & right, 97 left, 104, 108

Elton N. Woodbury, ©ATL Lepidoptera Research Fund: pp. 1 bottom, 3 top, 6, 14, 44, 54, 56, 58, 67, 68, 69, 70, 73 left & bottom right, 76 left, 77, 78, 79 left, 81 left, 84, 87, 88, 89, 90, 92, 94, 98 right, 99, 100 bottom, 101, 105

Oliver Yourke: Illustrations, pp. 27-31